Living with Palladio
in the Sixteenth Century

ANTONIO FOSCARI

LIVING
WITH PALLADIO
IN THE SIXTEENTH CENTURY

Translated by Lucinda Byatt

LARS MÜLLER PUBLISHERS

Jacopo and Francesco Bassano, *The Supper at Emmaus,*
1576–1577, Private collection

Living with Palladio in the Sixteenth Century

All the private buildings that Palladio designed for "Venetian nobles" and "gentlemen living on the mainland" are referred to as houses (*case*) in his writings.

While such an understatement might seem in contrast to the scale of his largest projects, the term was used by Palladio in homage to a political culture that was typical of Venice, where only one building could rightfully be named the "Palace". This was the palace that housed the governing bodies of the Republic.[1]

Moreover, there is another reason for calling these private buildings houses: having satisfied the requisite qualities[2] demanded by his high-ranking clients, these were structures that also had to be "suitable [today we might say convenient] for use by the family and household (*famiglia*)".[3]

Palladio's understanding prioritised the domestic functions of these private buildings, and in this respect he saw no difference between an urban house whose primary use was to allow a gentleman to participate in political life and a house on a country estate (*casa di villa*), which instead allowed him to manage his estates. The wording is very precise – a house built on an estate – and underlines his conviction that the building must be used "in the same way that it is customary in towns".[4]

What might well be expected of Palladio is that, having made this distinction, he would then describe the nature and composition of this unit, the family, for which the house became the expression, whether in the town or the countryside. Yet Palladio says very little about it. He only informs us that it is a hierarchical structure with the owner (*padrone*) at the top and at the bottom everyone involved in the everyday running of the household, the group Palladio calls the lesser household (*famiglia minuta*).

It is worth stopping to look more closely at this structure before we pay a "virtual" visit to the Palladian house built on the right bank of the Brenta for two brothers from the ducal branch of the Foscari family.

The first point to note is that Palladio takes for granted the fact that, in his day, a family of high social standing formed a group of persons who – as well as being bound by family ties – engaged in a specific trading activity or enterprise, and therefore comprised a unit that carried out an economic function of the kind undertaken by joint stock companies today. At the time it would have been inconceivable (and even Adam Smith would not yet countenance it in his brilliant *Inquiry into the Nature and Causes of the Wealth of Nations* of 1776) for a business to be managed with anything but private financial means.

Leaving aside this entrepreneurial concept of the family – an idea that was firmly rooted in the mentality of a society like that of Venice based on centuries of mercantile traditions – Palladio appears to give his

Jacopo Tintoretto and workshop, *Portrait of the family of Jacopo Soranzo,* c. 1551, Milan, Castello Sforzesco

own interpretation of a particular political and cultural trend that saw greater emphasis given in society to the landowner, namely to a gentleman who lived off his private assets and estates. To this extent the concept of family tended to be identified, in Palladio's mind, with the closest circle of the master's own relatives.[5]

Despite this Palladio never hints at the make-up of this family circle, nor does he mention the number of people who would have formed the *famiglia minuta*. This means that today – based on contemporary parameters – we might well think that, in both cases, there would only have been a few individuals.

Yet to convince ourselves otherwise we only need to reflect that Alvise Foscari's wife, Elisabetta Loredan, gave birth to eight boys and five girls, because – of the two brothers who commissioned Palladio – Alvise was the one who had undertaken to continue the family line. For this reason alone, a family unit of this size would have needed a household of at least twenty persons.

Vincenzo Coronelli, *Ca' Foscari, seen from the Grand Canal* and *Ca' Foscari, internal courtyard,* 18th century, Venice, Museo Correr

This is worth stating because – until a new generation of scholars engages in further research on these topics – it seems clear that a sixteenth-century seigneurial *house,* both in an urban setting and in the countryside, would have contained quite a large community and a varied one, not only in relation to the tasks, responsibilities and roles each individual member undertook but also in terms of their age, sex and social background. (Perhaps this explains why Palladio ideally compared a house to a "small city".[6])

Therefore, these houses – whether they were town houses or houses on country estates – were occupied with a level of intimacy that, for us today, can only be found if we step aside from the bourgeois canons introduced by the French Revolution. Moreover, this intimacy was only tolerated while the house was dominated – in theory, as well as in practice – by the figure of the master, whom Palladio placed at the head of the basic social structure he calls the *famiglia* or household.

In keeping with this interpretation, the houses built by Palladio were generally conceived as having "only one floor"[7] (the "main floor" [*primo ordine*]), in other words a single "beautiful and decorated" storey[8] which was "for the owner [...] to live in".[9] In fact, Palladio's main "concern" was to provide "accommodation for the owner",[10] whose rooms he describes as "the master's rooms"[11] (the "ground floor rooms"[12]).

That an external staircase was the only means of direct access to these apartments is not in itself surprising in the context of Venetian culture, given that in earlier times (and still in Palladio's day) the *piani nobili* of Venetian patrician houses were almost exclusively accessed by two flights of steps built within the high walls that enclosed the central courtyard.

Instead, in the *case di villa* designed and built by Palladio the stairs are positioned on a symmetrical axis to the house and are unprotected by other structures. As such they form a conceptual but also a physical link between the interior of the house and its surroundings. It is a link which Palladio emphasises, whenever possible, by building a road which projects the axis of symmetry through the house and into the landscape, and placing a loggia, a pronaos or a portico at the point where the axis intersects the house, thereby bringing the exterior and interior spaces of the house together.[13]

These elements alone provide sufficient grounds on which to recognise the enormous novelty of the Palladian villa. It is unprotected and indefensible. As such it is, or it wants to be, a sort of marker of acceptance, a celebration of that *pax veneziana* that the Republic had successfully brought about on the mainland after what had seemed like an unending period of war and turbulence.

Unprotected and indefensible: this also applies to the house built by Palladio "on the Brenta".[14] But it diverges from the scheme used in all the other *case di villa* he designed. Here, the house rises above a high basement and the portico, which stands above the basement almost like an acropolis, is not accessed by means of a staircase on axis with the symmetry of the building. This decision introduces a degree of detachment between the house and its surroundings and causes anyone who needs to climb up to the main floor to hesitate before choosing, wondering which of the two flights of steps placed on either side of the portico will lead to the level of the "master's rooms".

Another element, this time inside the house, helps to sanction the supreme dignity of the main rooms. The striking architectonic quality of the external stairs leading to the "master's rooms" are countered, in Palladio's buildings, by the restricted scale of the internal stairs which the architect defines as "smaller",[15] owing to the minimal measurements he gives them.

Such a striking difference between the external steps and these internal staircases depends on the subaltern role that Palladio gives to the two floors of the house which, not by chance, he defines in negative compared with the main floor. He writes that "the one underneath [...] and the one at the top [...] I do not define as a principal story (*ordine principale*) because neither lends itself to occupation by

Vincenzo Coronelli, *Palazzo Foscari, seen from the Brenta* and *Seen from the Garden* (comp.), from "La Brenta, quasi borgo ecc.", Venice, 1711

gentlemen".[16] It is on this basis that Palladio does not give any particular name to either of these two floors, nor does he specifically define their function, and instead he only talks about "the rooms at the bottom" (*stanze di sotto*)[17] and "the rooms above" (*stanze di sopra*),[18] sometimes referring to them simply as the "places" below and above.[19]

In order to overcome this reticence on behalf of the architect, let us walk, in our imagination, into the basement of the house. It contains all the functions linked to domestic management, which Palladio groups under the heading of essentials: "the cellars, the wood stores, the pantries, the kitchens, the smaller dining rooms (*tinelli*), the laundries, the ovens, and the other things".[20]

Not being able to give an antique example to underline the principle that those functions that we would now call "services" should be on a floor below the main floor (*ordine primo*), Palladio drew a comparison with the human body, taking it as the theoretical foundation for his choice, given that humanists had already used it as a conceptual model for architecture. Palladio replaced the principle of "imitating the Ancients" with that of "imitating Nature", and furthermore – suspecting that his readers would not be familiar with the theories elaborated by Leon Battista Alberti in this respect – he preferred to invoke divine authority as the creator of Nature and of the rules governing Nature.

"The reason is," he writes, "that since there are some noble and beautiful parts of the human body and some that are less pleasant and agreeable [...], we can nevertheless see that the former have an absolute dependence on the latter and cannot exist without them [without the less pleasant parts]; similarly too in buildings there must be some parts that are admirable and praiseworthy and others which are less elegant, without which, however, the former could not remain independent and thus would, in part, lose their dignity and beauty. But, just as our blessed God has arranged our own members so that the most beautiful are in positions most exposed to view and the more unpleasant are hidden, we too when building should place the most important and prestigious parts in full view and the less beautiful in locations concealed as far from our eyes as possible, because all the unpleasant things of the house are placed in them as well as all those that could be a nuisance and tend to make the most beautiful parts ugly."[21]

The deliberation, almost the insistence, with which Palladio justifies his choice to keep the essentials (*commodità*) on the ground floor of his *case di villa* – generally in the basement – is perhaps prompted by criticisms of a solution that weighed particularly heavily on many members of the *famiglia minuta*. Palladio was the first to admit that only where "the land [...] is cleansed of its damp and noxious vapours [...] [do] the inhabitants remain healthy, happy, and of good complexion".[22]

Even if, as Palladio specifies,[23] the *stanze di sotto* in the house built "on the Brenta" are not "partly underground",[24] or fully underground,[25] he nonetheless respects the principle that the essentials, namely the less attractive functions of the house, must be "concealed as far from our eyes as possible".[26] To achieve this, the windowsills of the rooms at the bottom are positioned quite high up compared with the level of the floor, so that anyone walking or standing outside the house cannot see what is happening inside these basement areas.

On the other hand, the fact that Palladio says nothing about a choice that to us may now appear rather surprising, namely that of having a granary above the owner's rooms, can be explained because to him, and to his contemporaries, it would have seemed quite obvious. It certainly was for his Venetian patrons, who for centuries had been accustomed to storing goods in the attics of their palaces-cum-warehouses in the city (*case-fondaco*) because keeping them on the ground floors, and not far above the water level of the lagoon, would have been impractical.

Perhaps there is also another reason for the lack of explanation. While it was undoubtedly true that each patron acquired an estate to increase his wealth by improving his property through his "skill in farming",[27] he did so against the background of an economic and political strategy that was regulated and supported by the Venetian magistracies. Therefore, the granary – the place where agricultural produce was accumulated – is an expression of the *raison d'être* of a house that was managed in keeping with the policies of the Republic.

Moreover, no other part of the house was more suitable than the "places above" for storing grains and also the beans and other vegetables that were harvested throughout the farming year. Not only were they well clear of the "dampness of the earth"[28] but they could also be more easily protected from thieves, given that there was only one way to get up to the attic, namely up the small staircase whose limited dimensions precluded any rapid escape. What was more, the owner could keep an eye on the staircase without stirring from his own rooms.

The specific use which Palladio attributes to the "places above" as granaries is confirmed not only by the remarkable roof trusses – which are visible in the same way as they are in many rural buildings – but also by the height at which the window openings are set compared with floor level (particularly in the first houses that Palladio built *in villa*). Indeed, the windows sometimes open at floor level in order to maximise the ventilation of the grain, which would been have stored loose on the floor. The use of the space is also confirmed by the broad bands of smooth plaster that cover the walls of these rooms up to a certain height above floor level, and around the doors. Mice that had climbed up this far, attracted by the scent of the grain and beans, were prevented by these smooth bands from evading capture by scrambling up the walls and hiding in the nooks and crannies of the roof timbers.[29]

The custom of using of the "places above" as a granary was already standard in the early Palladian *case di villa,* but it underwent a further evolution when Palladio's patrons entered more wholeheartedly into the role of agricultural entrepreneurs and their houses were transformed into fully fledged commercial centres, with the addition of adjoining farm buildings (the "barchesse"). It was for this reason that,

Agostino Gallo, "Carts" from *Le vinti giornate dell'agricoltura,* Venice, Borgomineri, 1584

Wooden roof trusses, Villa Foscari

The plaster bands preventing mice from climbing into the roof space, Villa Foscari

when commenting in his Second Book on some of his *case di villa,* Palladio calls the places above "mezzanines",[30] as if they were rooms with lower ceilings (like those created at this period in some Venetian palaces by "halving" the ground floors or the highest rooms). By doing so, he informs us that these spaces have acquired a more domestic function.[31]

When describing the house which is reflected in the waters of the Brenta (in which he was careful to include the smooth bands of plaster needed to prevent mice from escaping) Palladio goes a step further. Here, the *stanze di sopra* are explicitly described as rooms (*camere*), and they are given proper windows with windowsills at an appropriate height above floor level.[32]

That these *stanze di sopra* in the house built for the Foscari brothers were also potentially used for domestic purposes is also clear from a solution that is not present in any other Palladian building: namely the construction of two large dormers which shed ample light onto the large central space.[33] Another equally unique solution points to a similar conclusion: the presence in the smallest room of a fireplace (something that we would have expected to find in the smaller rooms on the main floor). The only explanation for such an unusual feature – enhanced on the exterior by the height and unique shape of its chimney – is the suggestion that this room was intended for the owner's young daughters who, as was customary at the time, were expected to live in a segregated part of the house under the careful watch of their nursemaids and to engage in the *skilled and beautiful art* of embroidery.[34]

The model of the human body used by Palladio when dividing the house into the first two storeys was retained when he then proceeded with a further division, creating two equal, specular sections. This was a necessary choice, he wrote, because "the whole body of the building would have an inherently suitable distribution of its members, making the whole beautiful and graceful".[35]

That Palladio respected this principle of symmetry in all his designs is well known. What deserves to

Battista Zelotti, *Holy Agriculture*, Villa Foscari

Jacopo Bassano, *Pastoral scene* (detail), c. 1560, Madrid, Museo Nacional Thyssen-Bornemisza

be highlighted in order to gain a clearer understanding is that he perceived it and tried to implement it in a much more radical way than anyone with an exclusively formal view of this principle.

If the two sectors of the house that are mirrored across the axis of symmetry of the building are to be compared with two organs of the human body, then for Palladio they must also function in a way that was wholly autonomous, as in the case of two eyes, two lungs, two kidneys. Palladio therefore describes each of these sectors as apartments (*appartamenti*). The word choice in Italian is particularly appropriate and confirms Palladio's intention that each of two heads of the family, whether alone or with his wife, could live apart (*appartare*), independent of the *famiglia* in the extended sense of the term.

In order to emphasise this intimate organisation of the "body of the building"[36] Palladio does not hesitate to repeat, whenever he gets the chance, that his buildings have two patrons not one, particularly the one erected at Malcontenta, where the patrons are two brothers with joint business interests (*comunione fraterna*).[37] Palladio somewhat self-indulgently also informs the reader that, as well as this *casa di villa*, the buildings for the Thiene family at Quinto, for the Pisani at Bagnolo, for the Barbaro at Maser and for the Thiene at Cicogna were also built for two brothers.

This is not to say that the house is not divided into two sectors if the owner does not have a brother with whom to share it. If this is the case, one of the two apartments is reserved for the owner's personal use while the other is reserved for his wife's use.[38] However, Palladio never mentions this form of symmetry because he is aware that, in practice, it is a form of homology, as Lévi-Strauss would later write in his *Myth and Meaning*. In the sixteenth century, however, society did not recognise any real parity in the roles played by men and women.

Each *appartamento* usually consists of three main rooms (*stanze prime*) and, ideally at least, the corresponding three rooms below (*stanze di sotto*). This shows how Palladio is convinced – and remains convinced throughout his life – that a layout of this kind is both fitting and sufficient for the needs of a gentleman, whatever his wealth and power. Moreover, there are a series of rational and also ethical reasons for following this rule, not least out of respect for the republican foundations of the Venetian political system which, even in buildings, forbad any form of self-celebration and any display of wealth that might create differentiation and hence divisions within the ruling class.

Even in the apartments reserved for each of the two brothers in the house "on the Brenta", Palladio sticks to the rule (which he learnt in his youth through the teaching of Gian Giorgio Trissino) that each should contain "large, medium-sized and small rooms, one side by side with the next, so that they can be mutually useful".[39]

In the same way as the reduced dimensions of the doors confirm the separation between each apartment and the central hall, which is the architectural fulcrum of the house, so the minimal width of the doors leading between the rooms in each apartment confirms that each room not only has its own, autonomous spatial identity but also a specific function.

In these three rooms, as Palladio points out, laying particular emphasis on each word, "one sleeps, eats, or receives guests".[40]

The room where "one sleeps" in the apartment is clearly the larger one, which Palladio describes as "large and spacious".[41] There is space for a bed without making the room feel cramped, since it needs to be used for different purposes at various times of day.

The *large room* in each apartment faces north, since this "would also contribute to comfort" in the summer, writes Palladio,[42] who appears to be thinking precisely of the large rooms in this house when he adds that the view over the river – the Riviera del Brenta in this case – "will also make it very cool in the summer and will be a lovely sight".[43]

Not that the large room would be any less comfortable in the spring and autumn months. A large

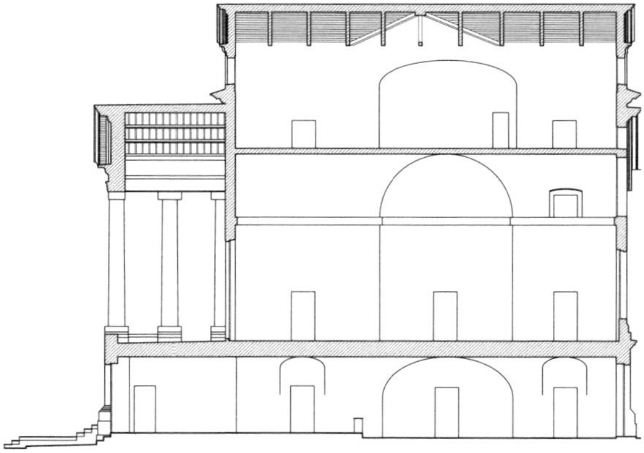

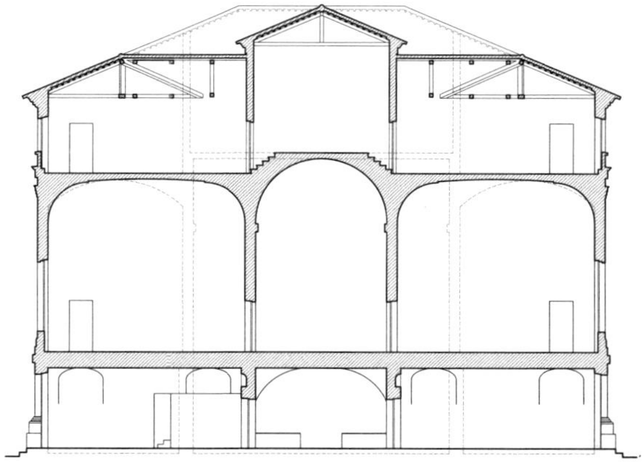

Cross section, Villa Foscari

Longitudinal section, Villa Foscari

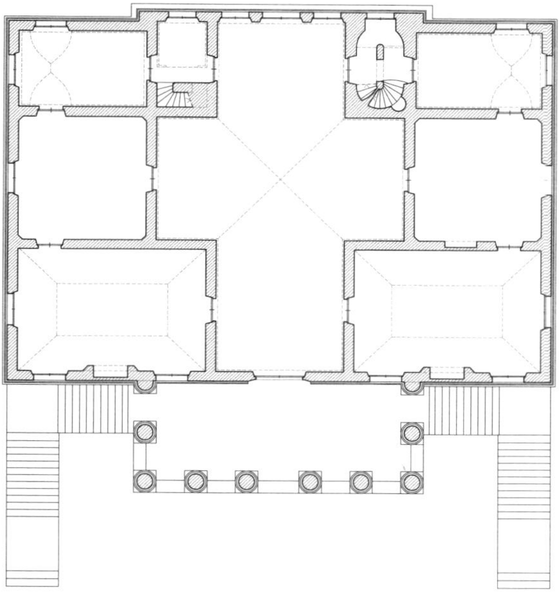

The plan's composition is symmetrical. The central hall, crossed longitudinally by the axis of symmetry, represents the unity of the family. Next to the central hall there are two distinct "appartments", each composed of three rooms: they are reserved for the two Foscari brothers who commissioned this building.

Plan of the main floor, Villa Foscari

 The small doors, Villa Foscari

"Roman" fireplace (without a projecting canopy) stands between the two north-facing windows, whose radiant heat will warm the bed facing it. The bed can also rely on the warmth of wall behind it, since the fireplace in the adjacent square room (*stanza quadra*) is on the other side.

The arrangement was different if the house was not lived in by two brothers (as was the case in the house on the Brenta when, after Nicolò's death, Alvise became the sole owner). In this case one of the two large rooms – the one facing east – was reserved for the owner's wife, who spent the time here with other gentlewomen and with her children's nursemaids, helped occasionally by some of the female servants. The other room, the one facing west, was kept for her husband's use, and when he wished to sleep with his wife he would send a page to summon her discreetly. We learn this from a figure which appears on the wall of the east-facing room and is echoed in the west-facing room by a portrait of Elisabetta Loredan, shown entering her husband's room and loosening her golden belt, a symbol of marital union (in the same way a wedding ring is worn by modern-day couples).[44]

Between the large room and the small room is a medium-sized room (*stanza mediocre*) with a square plan. As well as welcoming his relatives,[45] this is where the gentleman would receive "strangers", who might also be invited to spend the night.[46]

It is worth noting that the stranger (*forestiero*) referred to by Palladio was not just anyone. He was a learned man, probably of high social standing, who happened to be passing close by (in this case he might have been travelling along the Brenta on the *burchiello,* either towards Venice or from Venice to Padua), and as custom dictated, he would have paid a visit after presenting a letter of introduction from a common acquaintance.

It is also worth noting the care with which Palladio chooses the words to describe this rather abstract figure of the stranger, and the respect that he shows

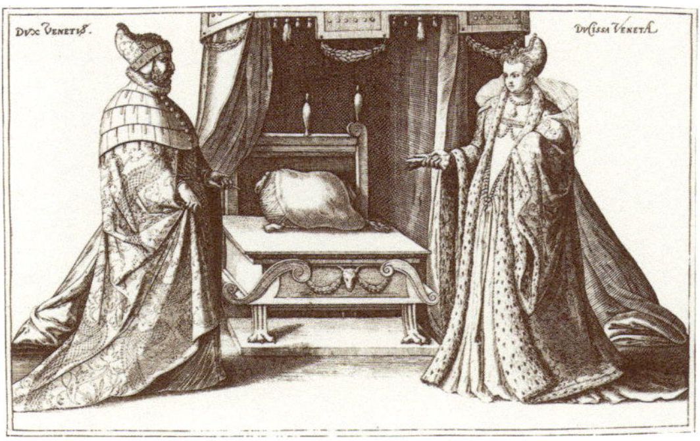

Giulio Coltri, "The Doge and the Dogaressa",
from *Habitus* by J.J. Boissard, 1581

for the political culture that was so strictly interpreted by the Venetian magistracies. These bodies always tried to pre-empt and even condemn any gathering of patricians held in a private setting, in one of their houses, given that this might give rise to cliques, lobby groups or other sorts of factions that could disrupt the political balances within the Palace, namely the Ducal Palace, where they were subject to strict electoral rules and procedures.

In order not to rule out the possibility that a Venetian gentleman might meet another patrician in his country house, Palladio was careful to clarify, in another passage in his *Libro Secondo,* that the owner of a house on a country estate (*casa di villa*) could entertain not only outsiders but also virtuous friends (*virtuosi amici*).[47]

Once again, Palladio surprises us with his precise choice of language. Here he evokes and combines two concepts: those of virtue and friendship, which had precise connotations in the culture of the day. Virtue was an ethical stance that the owner could and did exercise on his estate, "improving his property"

G. Grevembroch, *Varie Venete curiosità sacre e profane,* 18th century, Venice, Biblioteca Correr

*As you can also see on the following page the woman appears to be taller than normal as she serenely walks into her husband's large western room. Her height can be explained by the platform shoes (*zoccole*) used by Venetian women (and also the courtesans) in the sixteenth century.*
That this is Elisabetta Loredan, Alvise Foscari's wife, is clear from a series of explicit iconographical references.
She is wearing a married woman's gown and a string of large pearls which, by Venetian law, could only be worn by brides, and only in the early years of their marriage.
Elisabetta is unfastening a belt (in this case a golden belt) which was a symbol of conjugal union in the sixteenth century (in the same way that a wedding ring is today).
At end of the belt is a seal, which is clearly engraved with her husband's family coat of arms.
With the right hand, she points to a pendant in which, again, her husband's coat of arms may be impressed in wax: this symbolises the fact that Elisabetta is, like wax, perfectly moulded to the customs of the family into which she has married.

32 Battista Zelotti, *Elisabetta Loredan*, Villa Foscari

Battista Zelotti, *A Page,* Villa Foscari

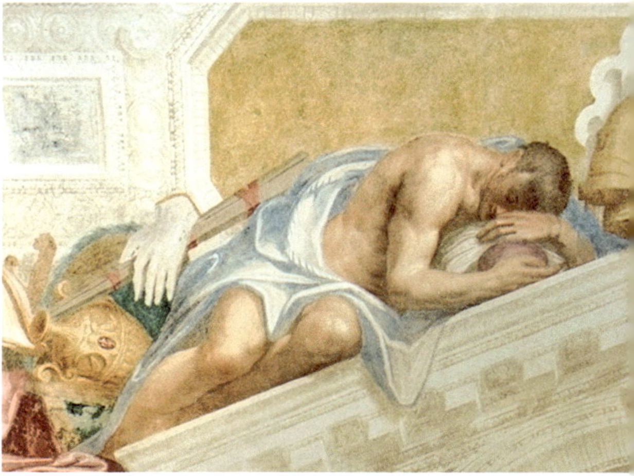

In the eastern room all the figures painted above the frescoed cornice are female, in order to signal that the eastern apartment is reserved for the use of Elisabetta Loredan, Alvise's wife. The figures in the corresponding large room on the western side, reserved for Alvise, are male.

Bernardino India, *Female figures,* Villa Foscari

Battista Zelotti, *Male figures,* Villa Foscari

through "his skill in farming"; and it was a value that – combined with the pleasure offered by "fountains and similar soothing locales"[48] – allowed those living on their country estates to "pursue that good life which they could enjoy there".[49]

By combining the concepts of virtue and friendship, Palladio cleverly rules out the possibility that the latter could be seen as being motivated by *utilitas* and therefore interpreted as a political activity. By giving preference to the Greek meaning of *philia*, Palladio also shows that he was aware of the interpretations of friendship advanced by Cicero in his treatise *De Amicitia*, a work that was circulated in the intellectual and political circles that Palladio frequented.[50]

But these were matters that, according to the strictly implemented laws of republican Venice, always ran the risk of being seen as potentially subversive. For instance, the Venetian magistracies would suspect one of Palladio's patrons of heresy: that unusual individual who received "all those who come to visit him" and invited them to spend the night – as Palladio himself notes – "in the room of the Virtue to which their dispositions appears to him most inclined".[51]

If either of the Foscari brothers had invited a friend to stay in their *casa di villa*, he would have given the visitor the *square room* of his apartment, where it is also possible that he too slept occasionally when he did not wish to sleep with his wife. If this was the case, then one of those "trestle-beds" would have been carried into the room, since we know that beds of this kind were kept in all patrician houses since they are included in the inventories drawn up following the death of the owner.

But let us come back to Palladio's own words. If the large room was used to sleep and the medium-sized room next to it was where the owner "receives guests", then, to follow the list of functions for each room in the apartment, the small room is where he "eats".

Initially, this affirmation is somewhat disconcerting because we are the products of a society where, for years, the concept of eating – namely lunching and dining – has been linked to that of the "dining room", turning the latter into a place, or a "structure", that celebrates the bourgeois concept of family.[52]

In a patrician house of the Cinquecento – whenever there was not a banquet (which would have been held in the portico or central hall of the house) – the *marenda,* a meal served in the morning, or the larger *desinar,* which was served at midday, and a light *cena* or supper in the evening (the French *soupper*), were eaten by the owner almost always alone, or more rarely, as far as we know, with his spouse. These meals were never eaten with the children, especially if they were adolescents.[53]

The bright light provided by the two large windows in the small room would certainly have enhanced the pleasure of eating there. Nor was the experience any less pleasurable because of the lack of a fireplace given that the "smaller rooms get warmer more readily than large ones"[54] if their external wall is exposed to the heat of the sun, as in the house by the river belonging to the Foscari brothers.[55]

The meal was served by a servant on a table supported by ordinary trestles. The "basic" nature of this solution was offset by the precious nature of the rug which was placed over the table, hanging down a little way on either side. A linen tablecloth, which was short enough to allow the rich border of the table-rug to be seen, was then laid on top. The cloth was starched and ironed in order to enhance the geometric pattern of its folds "into ordinary squares".[56]

But where could the gentleman, "whose spirit is tired by the aggravations of the city [...] attend in tranquillity to the study of literature and quiet contemplation"?[57]

These were activities that he would often undertake in the medium-sized room, given that his brilliant friends would only visit him on the rare occasions when they would entertain themselves together. Palladio tries to avoid uncertainties regarding how the house should be used, and therefore he suggests that the place where the owner could undertake intellectual pursuits is the study (*camerino*), which he creates above each small room on the main floor by

Venetian School, *The Supper at Emmaus* (detail),
16th century, Private collection

reducing the ceiling height. Palladio himself writes that "the small [rooms] should be divided up to create even smaller rooms where studies or libraries could be located".[58]

That these rooms might have been put to such an honourable use is confirmed by a line, which can still be seen on either side of the wall plaster. This line confirms that, in order to add dignity to the study – at least in the house which we are currently visiting – Palladio created quite a large wooden cornice at the top of the wall, and indeed we find this noted in a survey carried out by an attentive English architect in the eighteenth century.[59]

For the other brother who lacked either the vocation or the wish to spend his time in the country on "contemplative matters", Palladio took care to suggest an alternative use for the *camerino:* it could be used to keep "riding equipment and other tackle, which we need every day and which would be awkward to put in the rooms"[60] (in the other rooms on the main floor, he means).

Before we leave the three rooms that make up an apartment, we should note how all the rooms have windows with the same dimensions (a normal feature of Palladio's architecture) and yet the rooms have different levels of natural daylight depending on their size. The least light enters the large room, because two of its three windows face north (furthermore, one of them does not receive direct light because it opens within the portico); a medium level – albeit guaranteed by a single window – comes into the adjacent square room; while the small rooms is the brightest, with two windows (one facing directly south) whose dimensions are particularly large compared with the reduced room size.

While Palladio says nothing about what can be seen from the windows (except for briefly mentioning the "lovely sight"[61] offered by a river flowing in front of a house) not just because in the mid-sixteenth century the concept of landscape had not

The only tables to appear in the vast repertoire of sixteenth-century Venetian painting are those used to evoke biblical scenes, like the Last Supper and the Supper at Emmaus. The only biblical scene around a table that does not include the figure of Jesus is the banquet given by the rich man. In this painting Bonifacio de' Pitati depicts the rich man seated at a rug-covered table while he dines alone in the company of two courtesans and other musicians.

Bonifacio de' Pitati, *The Rich Man's Dinner* (detail),
c. 1535–1540, Venice, Gallerie dell'Accademia

Ludovico Pozzoserrato, *Concert in the countryside,* c. 1596, Treviso, Musei Civici

really matured, even in the minds of architects, but because in his *case di villa*, there was nothing to be seen in the distance other than an endless expanse of fields, practically bare of trees, with the odd thatched farmhouse, here and there, in which the peasants lived or kept their tools. Beyond these expanses of farmland, to the east and south of this house by the river, to which we are paying a "virtual" visit, lay the endless sandbanks and the lagoon waters. (This is the same view that continued to be documented in photographs from the first two decades of the twentieth century.[62])

It is also worth remembering that nothing could be seen of the surroundings while the windows of the house were shut. Flat or rather plate glass was not yet manufactured at the time, and only from the late eighteenth century onwards would it have allowed a clear view through the windows on windy days and during the winter months.

Therefore, during the day, daylight entered the rooms, when the windows were shut, through crown glass (vetri "a rullo") made by the master glassworkers of Murano by rapidly rotating the blowing iron which held the molten glass until the typical disc shape was formed by centrifugal force.

The question is, what happened when night fell? We do not know whether the shutters would have been closed at dusk in a *casa di villa* like this, because Palladio never mentions shutters in any of the *Books* (both because they are not really necessary,[63] and because these moving parts, made of wood that would have had to be painted – and therefore coloured – were not suited to the geometric rigour of a facade that aimed to conjure up the whiteness of the *opus quadratum* that appeared in Antiquity on the walls of the central body of the temple, the *cella*).

After sunset, however, the numerous activities concurrent inside the house gradually slowed down and finally came to an end. But it was not a sudden interruption, as we might think today, accustomed as we are to electric light supplied by mains power from

Jacopo Tintoretto, *Venus in the Mirror* (detail), c. 1578, Riverdale-on-Hudson, Stanley Moss Collection

power stations whose whereabouts we do not even know. In the kitchen, conversations may have continued for a long time around the fireplace while the flames slowly died down, in the pallid light of an oil-lamp hanging from the ceiling.

On the main floor above, it was possible to move around the rooms quite freely thanks to the lanterns hanging from rings deliberately set into the ceilings by Palladio himself. The owner might have consumed his evening meal under one of these lanterns, or may have continued to converse with his virtuous friend for a few hours after sunset.

Careful readers following this tour of the three rooms (plus the *camerino*) inside each apartment may have noticed an "emptiness" that we now need to address. The sole furnishings that have been mentioned so far are a bed (*lettiera*) in the large room and a simple table supported by wooden trestles in the small room.

Only the bed – with posts rising at all four corners – makes its presence felt, in its own way, also symbolically, because it is intended as a monument to the institution of marriage, or more precisely to female fertility. It is this interpretation that is almost always given to the presence of the Virgin Mary in the bedchamber, depicted as she hears the perturbing news brought to her by the archangel Gabriel.

But in normal life it is not the conception but the birth that is celebrated by this virtual domestic monument. It was here, as the wife lay in the bed after the birth, in a room that was sumptuously decorated for the occasion with the most valuable furnishings in the house, that all the relatives and acquaintances came to congratulate her. Indeed, this was one of the few occasions when a patrician's house was freely open to visitors and the Venetian magistrates would not intervene to suppress any undue influence.

In more prosaic terms, the bed is only a cubicle – a small room with a roof, protected on all four sides by hangings – and it assures its occupant or occupants a certain degree of privacy while maintaining a degree of warmth inside that, on the coldest days, would have been dispersed into the larger space of the main room.

At the sides of this cubicle are benches that open to store blankets, clothing and even valuable items, such as silverware that needed to be protected at night from the risk of theft. These low chests served as a step up and onto the bed itself – generally fitted with two layers of mattresses – but they also doubled as a hard surface that could be used by anyone lying in the bed.

Despite the elementary nature of its structure, even the trestle table on which the owner ate his meals had a certain symbolic value. This is ensured by the presence of the table-rug that was mentioned earlier. As an item of furnishing, its value enhances the majesty of the throne on which artists also painted the Madonna; the throne on which the assembled judges sit, inside a loggia, as they prepare to make a public declaration; carpets of this nature would also be hung by Venetian patricians over their balconies (*pergoli*) as a public statement of their wealth.

What else can we find in these rooms? Very, very few objects, as is demonstrated by the inventories that have survived. In addition to the trestle beds, which have already been mentioned, there would have been stools (or *panchette*), chairs and chests – many chests. These are the containers in which everything was stored, from clothes (which were far more precious than we can imagine today) and books to the documents that certified the family's ownership of properties and assets.

There were very few objects at the time that a gentlemen would have had around him. In the same way that the concept of landscape was in its infancy, there was also no conceptual category or practice that corresponded to what we now call furnishings. There were no wardrobes (*armadio, armoire*), as we understand them now, on the main floor: these are an innovation introduced during the course of the seventeenth century to store the "arms" that underpin

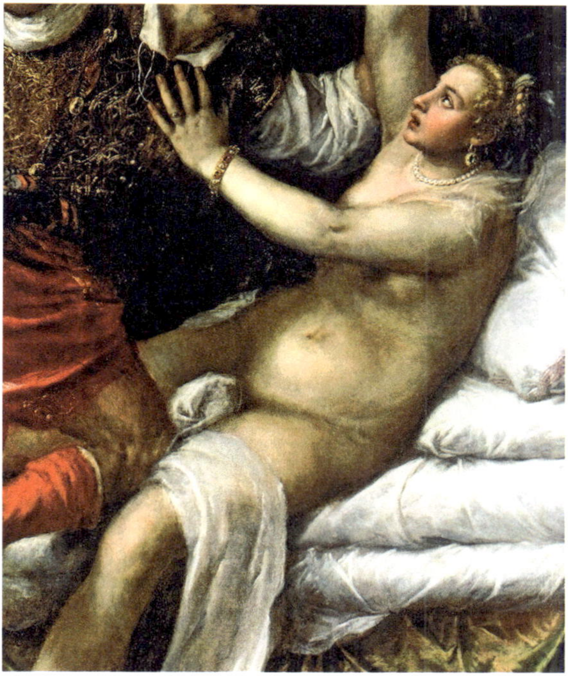

When Titian painted Lucrezia assaulted by Tarquin, the artist – who is a master of abstraction and reality – shows us how Venetian beds in the sixteenth century had two mattresses and a pile of cushions against which the occupant could lean while asleep.

Titian, *Tarquin and Lucretia,* 1571, Cambridge, Fitzwilliam Museum

Lambert Sustris, *Venus* (detail), c. 1540–1560, Amsterdam, Rijksmuseum

a civilisation, a feudal society, that was finally disappearing. There were no writing bureaus (*scrivania*): these were invented in the eighteenth century to demonstrate that the owner was a man who devoted himself to practical business and personally oversaw his estates. The furnishings of the dining-room, as we have already seen, were a nineteenth-century innovation, as well those furnishings designed for comfort (armchairs, divans, sofas, etc.).

The "emptiness" created by the absence of furnishings and objects is therefore dictated by social custom in the mid-sixteenth century. But it is a custom that Palladio skilfully interpreted to exalt the conceptual quality of his architecture. In the architect's vision, the walls and ceilings of his rooms must epitomise the whiteness of a material, namely lime, characterised by both its humble and extremely noble characteristics. In other words, they must display the whiteness that would allow the harmony of proportion between the measurements that defined the volume of these rooms to be perceived, and during daytime would reveal the changing colour of light on their walls.[64]

Jacopo Bassano, *Noah's Sacrifice* (detail), c. 1574, Potsdam, Stiftung Preußische Schlösser und Gärten

In the absence of furnishings, what brought these spaces to life were the figures painted using an "impoverished" technique (almost the only requirements for fresco painting were pigmented earths) that the new generation of artists knew how to practise with speed and modern *sprezzatura.*[65] In these ideally "Roman" spaces, these figures and figurative representations evoked the classical Roman myths, above all those narrated by Ovid with the brilliance that has immortalised his *Metamorphoses*. The stories – evoked in imaginative paintings – create a dialogue, and also disrupt the abstraction of an interior architecture in these Palladian houses that displays no ornamentation because it is wholly fulfilled by the rigour of its composition and the harmony of its spaces.

We must not be distracted by these figures which, like seductive sirens, try to make us linger as they entertain us on the main floor. Instead we will move down to the floor below: here the three rooms on the main floor correspond to three places (*luoghi*) – all of which are again interconnected – and the rooms

View of the central hall on the piano nobile, Villa Foscari

Battista Zelotti, *The Fall of the Giants*, Villa Foscari

 The spiral staircase, Villa Foscari

inhabited by the owner are dependent on these and "cannot exist without them".[66]

As if to make us understand his ability to move from the design of spaces with monumental scope to modelling spaces that are minimal to the point of being incompressible, Palladio leads us down to this floor by a circular staircase – a single flight of steps – that almost turns on itself, it is so narrow. But it is not on this proof of functionalism that we should focus, even though Le Corbusier was enthusiastic when he saw it.[67] Rather we should now walk into these "*luoghi*" or "rooms at the bottom".

The largest of the three – corresponding to the room on the piano nobile where "one sleeps" – has a large door that leads directly outside. The doorway is intended to stay open throughout the day because, otherwise, the light provided by the sole window, which is quite small, would not be sufficient.[68] These aspects alone convince us that this room acts as a sort of link between the interior and the exterior.

Inside all the tasks essential to the house are carried out, if necessary using the hooks Palladio expressly set into the barrel-vaulted ceiling: the pig would be butchered, plates would be washed using water from the river that flows alongside, knives would be sharpened, laundry would be washed here when it rained, as well the whole series of domestic tasks needed to meet the requirements of a household that – as we now know – would have been very large. Outside, wood was chopped for use in the kitchen and to heat the house; the laundry was hung out to dry in the sun; herbs and simples were grown as flavourings, and for the preparation of remedies.[69]

The second room (the one with the square floor plan that is below the medium-size room on the main floor) is the one in which one of Angelo Beolco's characters – often peasants tormented by a hunger so acute that any kind of food became a real obsession – could only dream of entering. We could liken the room to the Land of Cockaigne where food and drink abounded. Hanging from the ceiling hooks, in conditions of optimal ventilation and out of reach of cats

Francesco Valeggio (inc.: Stefano Mozzi Scolari),
Kitchen scene, 17th century

Activities inside the kitchen, from *Opera di M. Bartolomeo Scappi, cuoco,* Venice, Tramezzino, 1570

Activities outside the kitchen, from *Opera di M. Bartolomeo Scappi, cuoco*, Venice, Tramezzino, 1570

 The large room (western side), Villa Foscari

and dogs, were rows of peacocks, capons and hams. In the hearth, pigeons and various cuts of meat were slowly roasting, turning on spits operated by a roasting-jack that "turns by itself, by means of a wheel, with a mechanical escapement, like that of a clock".[70] On the walls, there was a "show" of plates and copper pans of all sizes, representing a universe of potential pleasures to satisfy any appetite.

It was here that women of all ages worked around a table where dough was almost always being kneaded and a variety of dishes were prepared, accompanied by the sound of their voices and the varying sounds of their tasks. Food was prepared and ingredients chopped, the most precious tableware and cutlery were washed in the sink, pans were scrubbed and polished, the fire was stoked and the embers raked, the pestle rhythmically pounded in the stone mortar beside the hearth, standing on a wooden log.

The owners' children often played here with the cats, when they were young; tugging at the skirts of the kindest and most cheerful countrywoman (*donna di villa*), perhaps one who was already getting on in years. The young girls learnt how to sew and embroider. The fire was always lit. (It takes at least three-quarters of an hour to cook polenta over the fire in the *caliera,* the large pan used for this purpose, which hangs from a chain suspended from the chimney breast).

Silence only falls on this square room when the owner's wife walks in – and this may happen more than once a day. She comes to inspect the vegetables, fruit, meat and fish which have been brought here by the tenant farmers or from the market, to check the quality and the prices, and then to decide when and how to prepare them.

Walking through the kitchen, filled with the appetising smell of cooking, as well as heat and the sound of voices, we enter a small room which is brightly lit from two windows. This is the *tinello,* or small dining hall, where the owners' children eat their meals – perhaps on a rota – with their tutors, and occasionally

View of the central hall on the ground floor, looking north,
Villa Foscari

Jacopo Tintoretto, *Venus in the Mirror* (detail), c. 1578,
Riverdale-on-Hudson, Stanley Moss Collection

also the owner himself when he feels the need for their company. Its vicinity to the kitchen means that the food is served piping hot, as Leon Battista Alberti had rightly advised his educated readers.[71]

The rays of the sun on the outside wall of this room and the warmth of its inner wall, which is heated by the fire burning in the kitchen hearth, means that the *tinello* is always pleasantly warm, even during the autumn months when the air begins to cool. If the owner or a relative ever wished to take a bath, it would be here in this room, in a tub filled with hot water carried through from the kitchen next door.

The fact that Palladio does not mention this, and more to the point, does not include any structure or plans for a bathroom in any of his projects; and the fact that he never hints at these customs anywhere in the *Four Books,* or show any baths or swimming pools in the many drawings left by him of antique Roman baths clearly depends on his strict compliance with contemporary theories of hygiene. Based on these, the dilation of the pores resulting from contact with water, above all hot water, made the body permeable to many diseases, including the plague, which most then believed to be transmitted through the air. Therefore, there was only one solution for keeping the body clean: it had to be vigorously rubbed, while dry. The only remedy for the drawbacks of such a basic level of hygiene was – for those who could afford it – to use perfumes. A large copper perfuming pan (*profumiere*), with a long wooden handle, was even inserted between the bed coverings.

Confirmation that this, rather than any form of modesty, was the reason why Palladio did not mention the subject of baths comes from his insistence and the lack of embarrassment with which he draws his reader's attention in *Book Two* to the latrines (*necessari*). He states repeatedly that the latrines must be enclosed within the walls, or in the stair well, arguing that the draught, naturally created in staircases, will guarantee that bad smells are rapidly extracted from the house.

Palladio does not include a bathroom in any of his projects (nor does he mention the presence of swimming baths in his reconstructions of Roman baths), and in the same way no contemporary is ever portrayed washing in sixteenth-century Venetian art. The only scenes of bathing figures are biblical ones: Bathsheba (whose nudity is spied on by King David) and Susanna (who is watched by the "elders").

Jacopo Tintoretto paints Susanna as she emerges from the bath and he also shows her with a mirror, a comb, a perfume bottle and a small ointment jar.

Jacopo Tintoretto, *Susanna and the Elders* (detail), 1555,
Vienna, Kunsthistorisches Museum

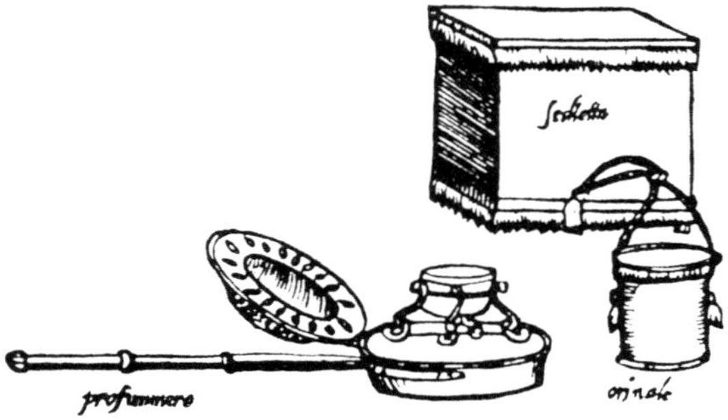

Commode, urinal and perfume burner, from *Opera di M. Bartolomeo Scappi, cuoco,* Venice, Tramezzino, 1570

After being used, the circular opening of a latrine (which on one occasion Palladio also calls a lavatory or *cesso*[72]) is closed with a wooden lid. Vents, which Palladio calls *spiragli,* were usually inserted in the thickness of the walls and were designed to let out the bad smells from the pit placed at the bottom of the stairs.[73] In the house on the Brenta, as in his other buildings,[74] the lavatories and vents are set into the gap created between the circular wall enclosing the spiral staircase and the orthogonal frame of walls inside which the staircase is built.

In terms of hygiene this is an avant-garde solution that is not present in many other houses from the sixteenth century. But it did not mean, also for reasons of privacy that this solution does not address, that the owner and his wife no longer followed the customary practice of keeping a seggetta, or commode in their large room, as well as a urinal of the kind illustrated by Bartolomeo Scappi in the treatise he published in 1570.[75] Servants would have been charged with emptying and cleaning these receptacles on a regular basis.

View of the east facade, Villa Foscari, c. 1932

But without dwelling on the stairs or in the large rooms, let us return our attention to the basement.

There is no evidence at this level, nor does it seem likely, that there was a division into two distinct sectors as we saw on the *ordine primo* or main floor. Palladio was well aware of what Leon Battista Alberti had written, over a century earlier, in the Third Book of his treatise *De Familia.*[76] "[A]t two tables, two tablecloths are spread, two hearths consume two piles of logs, two households need two servants [...] To make two families out of one requires double expense."[77] So what use was made of the three rooms on the side of the house opposite the kitchen that we described earlier?

We can only be reasonably certain of one thing as we move around inside the house, namely that the large room was used – at least from a certain time onwards – as a wine cellar. There are three good reasons for this: the fact that it faces east (Palladio says that the cellars "must receive light from the east");[78] that

Paolo Veronese, *Carriage* (detail), c. 1560, Maser, Villa Barbaro

"the floor is made of terrazzo", which Palladio recommends for a cellar;[79] and, lastly, that the door that connects this room to the outside was altered at some stage (as can be seen in an old photograph) to allow larger barrels to be carried in whose diameter exceeded the width of the door.

To judge by Palladio's own words, since he talks of *tinelli* (in the plural) when he lists the essentials provided on the ground floor, we should understand that the central room – the square room corresponding to the kitchen on the opposite side of the house – might have been used for meals at midday and in the evening by Alvise and Elisabetta's numerous children.

Yet, we can also offer a different interpretation if we remember – as has already been said – that the lower floor is not underground or semi-underground, as it is in all the other Palladian villas. In addition, its ceilings are much higher than in any other Palladian *casa di villa*. Taking both these factors into consideration and linking them to the fact that, during the course of the seventeenth and eighteenth centuries

Vittorio Zonca, *Il carro di Fusina*, from *Nouo teatro di machine et edificii per uarie et sicure operationi*, Padua, Pietro Bertelli, 1607

(the only ones for which we have reliable information), this unique building was always called "palazzo", we realise that the central room on the ground floor with its independent access from the outside through a large doorway can be likened to an "entrance", similar to those designed by Palladio for his town houses, or "palaces".

This conclusion can only be drawn in the light of two other aspects: the first is the architectural quality of the southern facade onto which the doorway opens; the second is the fact that there is a straight path leading to this doorway, which runs precisely along the building's axis of symmetry. Therefore, this central room, with its unique architectural qualities, can be thought of as "the first part [...] which anyone entering the house is presented with"[80] coming from the land; in other words, this is a "land entrance".

These entrances are "public places and serve as a place where those waiting for the master to come out of his lodgings can stand to greet him and do business with him".[81] The master of this house on the river, Alvise Foscari,[82] a man intensely engaged in the

Vincenzo Coronelli, "Burchiello che viaggia sopra la Brenta", from *La Brenta, quasi borgo ecc.*, Venice, 1711

official activities of the Republic, was someone who would have often have been met, because he frequently passed through this entrance on his way to the ducal palace, seat of the magistracies with whom he had almost daily commitments.[83]

He went through this entrance because it was often easier to ride to Fusina by horse ("which we need to every day"[84]) and then take the boat to Venice, rather than take a boat down the Brenta, which flowed straight past the house. Not only could a good horse go considerably faster than a gondola or the burchiello, which only travelled at three miles an hour as Goldoni informs us, but also the process whereby flat-bottomed Venetian boats were hoisted over the embankment that separated the Brenta from the lagoon (in a machine known as the carro) could lead to delays in the event of heavy traffic.

While we should regard it as an entrance, this central room did not solely have a representative function, similar to the hallways (*androni*) in the town houses owned by patrician Venetian merchants, where for centuries bags of spices, fabric bales and numer-

Barbara and Antonio Foscari on a gondolino in front of the Villa

ous other goods purchased in the East had been unloaded, destined for markets throughout Europe. It was therefore natural that a Venetian patrician – accustomed to this interplay between his political and social life and business – would allow the laughter or curses of the *famiglia minuta* to mingle and echo under the vaulted ceilings of the ground floor, in the same way that he would store in the villa sacks of grain and bags of beans that porters (*bastasi*) would carry on their shoulders up to the top floor, where they could be stored in drier conditions, and bring downstairs again when it was time to load them onto the barge to take to the Rialto market.

In a setting like this it would seem likely that the square room adjacent to this central space (and its corresponding one on the floor above, where the owner received his brilliant friends) was where the *degano*, the administrator who oversaw the household, and the factors (*gastaldi*) who ran the farming activities were based. It was here that they monitored all these operations and undertook a variety of administrative tasks, including the tricky job of checking the estate boundaries; managing relations with the tenant farmers; keeping a record of gifts (*regalie*); taking on seasonal women workers; and, in short, keeping an eye on the world that revolved around a large house like this.

When the owner was resident in the villa he would walk from this square room into the *camerino* in order to monitor these movements: it was a small room, well lit by two large windows, preceded by a sort of antechamber (where he would keep the saddle and other riding "tackle" which, as we already know, "would be awkward to put in the rooms" on the main floor[85]).

Here, the experts from the Magistracy of Waters would meet to discuss the reclamation operations that Alvise Foscari was carrying out on his estates, or to settle the dispute that had arisen owing to the occupation of the lagoon foreshores undertaken by his uncle Jacopo about twenty years earlier in order to start breeding cattle.[86] The *padrone* would also have continued to use this *camerino* for his meetings with the Capitano of Gambarare, who also had a property "on the Brenta" a little further to the west, or with the notary whom he summoned to draw up purchase agreements for farmland, or with the village priest of Gambarare[87] and other owners of neighbouring estates.

It is not hard to imagine the axis of the path, first leading up to the southern facade of the house, then running longitudinally through the house and out of the northern end, through the thickness of the basement below the *portico* and through a doorway that is similar in size to the one on the southern side, before ending at the banks of the Brenta where we can visualise a boat moored to the jetty.

The door opposite to the one we have called the "land entrance" is therefore, ideally, a "water entrance". This was where the palace official most probably arrived to consult the patrician on matters of state, or the stranger who, finding himself on the Brenta, came to visit him. If either of them had to wait they would have been accommodated in one of the two square rooms – each of which was well lit by three windows – that Palladio created in the basement area under the portico.

Given that we have drawn attention to the figure of the stranger arriving in front of the house for the first time, let us try to put ourselves in his shoes and imagine his amazement when he saw a building like the one reflected in the waters of the Brenta, whose imposing outline is not always easy to interpret, even centuries later.

Before disembarking he would have seen an architectural form that he could not have seen anywhere before. An Ionic hexastyle portico projecting from the facade of a private building is the epitome of a *novitas* that overturned century-old cultural patterns.

It would not have helped our stranger that, in order to overcome the subjection – not to say awe – instilled by such a paradigmatic building, he had to move away from the building's axis of symmetry and decide which of the two specular staircases to choose in order to climb up to the portico, a structure whose height alone appeared to set it apart from any direct relationship with the "public".

There are other reasons, too, why the floor level of this portico – unlike those we find in all other Palladian buildings – does not mediate between the exterior and interior of the house. Because it is surrounded on three sides by solid columns and topped by an impressive lacunar ceiling, it tends to be seen by anyone standing in front of the house as a tribune (a *tribunale*, as the Venetians would have said at the time). The elevated status of anyone standing on this tribune, between its two central columns, is enhanced by the large "all'antica" doorway visible behind them, which leads into the central room.

Stepping through this doorway, and leaving the north-facing (and often shaded) portico behind him, the visitor is struck by the overhead light which floods through many windows that form an immense opening above the central room on the side opposite

View of the northern facade, Villa Foscari

the portico. As the emotion aroused by such a surprising architectural message gradually fades, our virtual stranger starts to perceive how Palladio manages to dilate and contract these spaces, ideally evoking the typology of the ancient Roman baths from which the architect also took the cross vaults that arch over this room and the singular window right at the top of the series of openings, which imbue the space with almost blinding brilliance.

Moving around inside the house, we have been able to see how Palladio was careful to avoid any precise definition of the composition of a patriciate household, the relationship between the owner and his collaborators and the lower household (*famiglia minuta*), his intimate relations with his spouse, and the way he behaved towards his younger children and unmarried daughters. We have also seen how also in his use of words (like "house", "stranger", "friendship"), Palladio takes particular care not to take positions that could, or even might depart from the norms governing the political culture of the Republic.

It is not unexpected therefore that he says nothing about the function, or the possible ways of using the surprising room which is also the symbolic centre of this house. With striking parsimony he gives merely a geometrical description which can only really be appreciated by an expert in architecture. "The vault of the hall", he writes, "is a semicircular cross vault and its impost is as high above the ground as the hall is broad".[88] More generally – in a paragraph in *Book Two* which introduces the subject of central halls in his *case di villa* – he simply notes that this was where "those waiting to greet the master of the house or to ask him for some help or a favour can spend their time pleasantly".[89]

To guide our understanding of how this central hall might have been used, and in the absence of documents, we can turn to the lesson offered last century by Diaghilev who listened to Rossini's music in this room while lying on a sofa so low that it seemed more like a mattress on the floor, or by Serge Lifar

View of the entrance doorway to the piano nobile,
Villa Foscari

NON MOLTO lungi dalle Gambarare ſopra la Brenta è la ſeguente fabrica delli Magnifici Signori Nicolò, e Luigi de' Foſcari. Queſta fabrica è alzata da terra undici piedi, e ſotto ui ſono cu cine, tinelli, e ſimili luoghi, & è fatta in uolto coſi di ſopra, come di ſotto. Le ſtanze maggiori hanno i uolti alti ſecondo il primo modo delle altezze de' uolti. Le quadre hanno i uolti à cupola: ſopra i ca merini vi ſono mezati: il uolto della Sala è à Crociera di mezo cerchio: la ſua impoſta è tanto alta dal piano, quanto è larga la Sala: la quale è ſtata ornata di eccellentiſsime pitture da Meſſer Battiſta Venetiano. Meſſer Battiſta Franco grandiſsimo diſegnatore à noſtri tempi hauea ancor eſſo dato prin cipio à dipingere una delle ſtanze grandi, ma ſopraueuuto dalla morte ha laſciata l'opera imperfetta. La loggia è di ordine Ionico: La Cornice gira intorno tutta la caſa, e fa fronteſpicio ſopra la loggia, e nella parte oppoſta. Sotto la Gronda vi è vn'altra Cornice, che camina ſopra i fronteſpicij: Le camere di ſopra ſono come mezati per la loro baſſezza, perche ſono alte ſolo otto piedi.

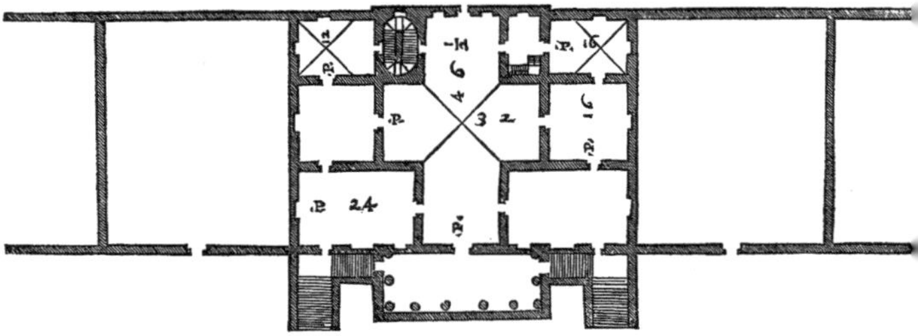

Andrea Palladio, *I Quattro Libri dell'Architettura*, Venice, Francesco de' Franceschi, 1570, *Libro Secondo*, p. 50 (comp.).

who danced barefoot here at dusk by the light of a few candles.[90] Diaghilev and Lifar had understood that music and dance are pertinent – we might even say congenial – artforms that belie the enigmatic quality of these spaces.

Palladio, the grand master of silence, says nothing of music and dance, although we can be certain that he drew on contemporary music theories for those rules of proportion that give his buildings that *Visible Harmony*[91] which is such a distinct characteristic of the rooms in this house. We can also be sure that Palladio not only knew the few passages on music written by Vitruvius but that he also followed Daniele Barbaro in an effort to give an acceptable interpretation to these words (without disguising the fact that he did not agree with them).[92] What is more, Palladio must surely have known the chapel master of St Mark's Basilica who was completing his work on the most advanced theoretical analysis of music, the *Istitutioni harmoniche,* precisely at the time this house was being built.[93]

Palladio disregards the topical nature of these debates and, as in the case of architecture, he again anchors music, which is seen as an autonomous discipline, to Antiquity. In doing so he links music, both in theory and in practice, to the example of the great Roman intellectual Boethius who, in his interpretation of Greek tradition, had ranked Music as one of the "sciences" of the Quadrivium. This explains why Palladio had no trouble in accepting Music, or its ideal representation, together with the figures of Astronomy, Mathematics and Geometry, in one of the "excellent paintings"[94] executed by Battista Zelotti above four of the six doors facing into the hall.[95]

But it was not just to avoid any "mannerist" implication, also for Music, that Palladio maintained this prudent approach. It seems likely that once again he was interpreting the customs of the Venetian Republic. Palladio therefore rules out the possibility, described by Baldassarre Castiglione when writing of a courtly setting, where "I am not satisfied with our Courtier unless he be also a musician, and unless, besides understanding and being able to read music, he can play various instruments."[96] Nor would Palladio have acknowledged Castiglione's affirmation that "if we rightly consider, no rest from toil and no medicine for ailing spirits can be found [...] than this",[97] or that of Daniele Barbaro, which is almost identical in substance, that different forms of music "will delight the wearied intellect of men and supply gentle instruction for life".[98] Palladio bypasses the subject, and for him, as we have already seen, only the study of literature and quiet contemplation on the country estate provide solace "for one whose spirit is tired by the aggravation of the city".[99]

But perhaps another factor may account for Palladio's prolonged silence, which, at this point, seems like reticence. If he had even hinted at music, he would have brought into the house – at least in theory – a female figure to whom he never refers in his *Books* (except once when he says that the patron's wife can live in her own apartment at the back of the house).[100] Contrast this with Baldassarre Castiglione, an intellectual who belonged to the generation before Palladio, who had not hesitated to affirm, "it is no wonder that in both ancient and modern times [women] have always been particularly fond of musicians, finding music a most welcome food for the spirit".[101]

If music was performed in a domestic setting – which Castiglione hints at – there are understandable grounds for the criticism made by Gioseffo Zarlino of the fashion ("as is done at present", he writes) of organising musical performances with "multiple parts, and many singers and instruments". Music should be performed "with discretion (*giudizio*)", and the master of the Doge's chapel stresses that "singing to the sound of the lyre or the lute" is more in keeping with the custom of the Ancients, who advocated simplicity.[102] This, therefore, is what we presume may have happened in a Palladian house on a country estate, "reciting some beautiful, learned and elegant Poetry accompanied by some instrument".[103]

Battista Zelotti, *Bacchus and Ariadne*, Villa Foscari

Battista Zelotti, *Concert*, Villa Foscari

In this painting Titian ironically evokes the debate about the superior quality of music from stringed instruments compared with wind instruments. Because wind instruments were played with the mouth, their music was unable to temper the erotic effects of the music with words and the expression of moral concerns. Here Cupid whispers to Venus and the musician is distracted while he plays the organ.

Titian, *Venus with an organist and Cupid*, 1555, Madrid, Museo del Prado

But if we turn to the decorative cycle on the walls of this house, we realise that the owner – who played a decisive role in defining the fresco programme – also had different views of the symbolic meaning or effects of music. He decided that a truly surprising number of musical instruments of all kinds should be depicted on the walls of the room used by his wife, as if to entertain her in style: a cornet, a flute (*traversiere*), a recorder (*flauto a becco*), a clarinet (*tromba naturale* or *tromba chiarina*), an oboe and other trumpets, just to mention the wind instruments. But also a bass viol held between the legs (*lirone*), a guitar, two lutes, a small viol (*viella*), a *viola da braccio* (held in the arm), an English cithara (*cetra inglese*) as string instruments; and a tambourine with jingles as a percussion instrument.[104] In all, it is a collection unparalleled in any other contemporary decorative cycle.

Moreover, in the square room of the patron's own apartment, where he clearly planned to welcome friends who were not only "virtuous", music is evoked as an art that arouses erotic; pagan-like; and, in short, Dionysian qualities.

On the ceiling of the virtual pergola, inside the bower of vine tendrils from which hang bunches of ripe grapes, we find Bacchus, in his radiant prime, clasping Adriane to him. Beyond the pergola, which is enclosed at the bottom by a balustrade, on one side we see a pagan sacrifice and on the other a concert scene, in which the presence of a chubby cupid at the feet of the musicians is enough to explain the erotic effect that was expected of music.

Dance, too – another custom on which Palladio remained completely silent – could arouse excitement akin to the Dionysian rites, so much so that in 1549 Simeon Zuccolo attacked this custom, which was rapidly spreading throughout the Veneto, with as much fury as he could muster in a printed pamphlet titled The Madness of Dance (*La Pazzia del Ballo*).[105] But once again, as had happened after the moralising stance taken by Gioseffo Zarlino on music, a counterattack was printed, by a prelate of all people, the Bishop of Strongoli, Rinaldo Corso, who in his *Dialogo del Ballo*[106] asserted that dance, like music and architecture, was governed by “secret harmonic numbers”.[107] What was more, dance could be seen as the art of good conduct and persuasion, given that “through Dance, like a good teacher, we learn noble movements of the body, and consequently how to bow with greater dignity, how to turn more gracefully, and how to attract the souls of others using a variety of pleasing movements”.[108]

For a lively account of this custom we can turn to a few lines written by the famous architect’s son Francesco Sansovino regarding the etiquette for introducing a *novizia* (a prospective bride) to her new relatives and friends at a ceremony held in her father’s house. The dance master (maestro di danza) “leads the bride out of a room, dressed traditionally in white and wearing her hair loose, hanging down to her shoulders, threaded with gold braid. And once the ceremonious words of marriage have been pronounced, she is led around the room, to the sound of pipes, trumpets and other harmonious instruments, all the time dancing calmly and curtseying to the guests”.[109]

Little or nothing is known about the use of dance, accompanied by chords played on an instrument – often a psaltery (*salterio*) or harpsichord – save for the evidence provided by the works of a Netherlandish painter, Lodovico Pozzoserrato (Lodewijk Toeput), who became, to a certain extent, the bard of Venetian villa culture. In the same way, we would know little or nothing of how feasts and banquets were organised if there had not been a patrician who understood the cultural importance of these customs, also because of his own enjoyment of them. Although the Venetian magistracies suspected them and often prohibited them, the diarist in question regarded them as an expression of civilisation whose real nature and complexity had to be viewed as a whole, even in its most social aspects.

On the subject of banquets, without Marin Sanudo’s valuable *Diaries*[110] we would know nothing of the magnificent banquet held for Ferigo’s wedding in

May 1515 after a memorable theatrical performance, at which the actors, including some dwarves, recited poems in different languages. The banquet was given in the *casa grande* belonging to the Foscari family in Venice and Ferigo would become father to the two brothers who later built the *casa di villa.* Among the 420 guests, there were ninety-six women. All the guests were seated. The ambassadors for the Spanish king, the pope and the King of Hungary dined, using silver cutlery and tableware, in a separate room with the doge's three sons (the bride's cousins) and a number of other leading patricians.[111]

Nor would we know about the banquet for 400 guests invited by the San Simeon branch of the Foscari family to welcome a member of the ducal family of Mantua, Federico Gonzaga, to Venice in 1520. On this occasion as well, the festivities followed a series of spectacular events, partly public and partly private, including Ruzzante's first performance in Venice. Unlike the banquet for Ferigo's wedding, which had taken place on the piano nobile of the *casa grande,* this was held on the first floor of a "theatrical structure" which the Foscari of the San Simeon branch had built beside their family house where Doge Francesco Foscari was born in 1373.[112]

After Marin Sanudo died in 1536 we find almost nothing more that was written with the same precision and lucidity about events in which politics and culture, experimental performances and various other fashions are so inextricably linked. In particular, we have no more descriptions of banquets, except for the canvases of Paolo Veronese, usually painted on a large scale, hanging where no one would ever have expected to find them. A particularly renowned case is the huge painting that appears on the end wall of the refectory of the Benedictine monastery of San Giorgio Maggiore. In it Veronese – in open disagreement with Palladio who had built this refectory – portrays the most profane event Jesus ever attended, the *Wedding Feast at Cana,* as a sumptuous social occasion where superbly dressed women, seated at tables laded with the most expensive dishes, seem overwhelmed by the crowds of fellow guests and

Entertaining dances in a Venetian garden, 16th century

Hic Antenorei Connubia magna Senatus,
Patriciésq vides cœtus, Venetésq Hymenæos:
Et celebres thalami ritus tędásq iugales
Solennésq vrbis pompas, claroésq triumphos:

Teodoro Bernard (inc.: Giulio Goltzio),
Patrician weddings, 16th century

the sound of sophisticated musical instruments, while a few dogs scavenge for scraps at the diners' feet.

In Palladio's day, however, events of such importance were not held in a house on a country estate because in the mid-sixteenth century the fashion of "villeggiatura" had not yet become established. Only a few decades later many Venetian patricians would indeed furnish their *case di villa* with grand reception rooms.

But we can be certain that banquets and dinners were also held here (even if Palladio is also completely silent on this point) because a farm provides many different sorts of produce: not only vegetables, eggs and fresh milk, but also fish and meat in this case given that the estate is almost on the edge of the lagoon and also farmed cattle. Furthermore, it is important to remember that this was a period when culinary art was so appreciated that a leading cook would shortly be able to describe it as a genuine "learning" (*dottrina*), and what was more, "exceptional learning".[113]

Culinary art had reached such a level of specialisation that it required countless utensils and pieces of equipment, like those carefully documented in the treatise of another famous cook, Bartolomeo Scappi.[114]

On the subject of utensils, and talking of banquets, let us return to the ground floor where all the produce required to prepare the dishes were delivered and stored, depending on the season, and where the cooks would oversee their preparation, assisted by varying numbers of attendants and servants.

While the cooks were busy on the floor below, on the main floor, namely in the apartment used by the owner, large numbers of trestle tables were assembled to form a long table and the temporary backdrops to the meal were constructed – the sideboards (*piattaie*) and table for bottles (*bottiglierie*) – transforming the banquet into an event that resembled a performance.

The table may perhaps also have been set in the portico of the house, given that sixteenth-century paintings of banquets – except for those of the Last Supper – show that it was commonplace in the

Veneto for events like this to be held in loggias. But when a large number of guests were invited, the only option would have been the central hall. The table was set along the axis of symmetry of the hall, to make it as long as possible. The sideboard and the drinks table were probably positioned at the sides of the two cross-wings, to give free access to the square rooms at the sides, where distinguished guests could sit (as happened in the house in Venice on the occasion of Ferigo's marriage).

Rugs were laid over the tables, as we already know, and they were then partially covered with carefully starched tablecloths. The tables were then laid with tableware and cutlery (including those forks that were so still little known in Europe), as well as decanters and glasses of various types made by the master glass-workers on Murano.

Although the number of guests invited to *casa di villa* was lower than could be invited to a house in Venice, we should not conclude that a banquet resembled a modern-day dinner party, however sumptuous. It was an event that involved a large number of people[115] – whether guests, valets, musicians or servants – and there would also have been acquaintances present as spectators standing around the table. This was in every sense a spectacle in which everyone (or almost everyone) was both actor and audience.

The actors included the guests seated at the table: ladies and gentlemen who showed off their magnificent clothing and their appreciation of the new forms of conduct that had been recently codified by Monsignor Della Casa in his book *Galateo.*[116]

The dramatic entrance of the steward (*scalco*), the cupbearer (*coppiere*) and the carver (*trinciante*) was also carefully staged, and they had to demonstrate their specialised skills and dexterity. Likewise, the *credenziere* who was in charge of the sideboard or *credenza* and those who served and changed the plates (*soprastante al piatto*) played a similarly theatrical role. The carver, in particular, played a particularly dramatic part in carving the meat "all'italiana", or in the Italian way, holding the roast at arm's length on

Paolo Veronese, *The Wedding Feast at Cana* (detail), 1562–1563, Paris, Louvre

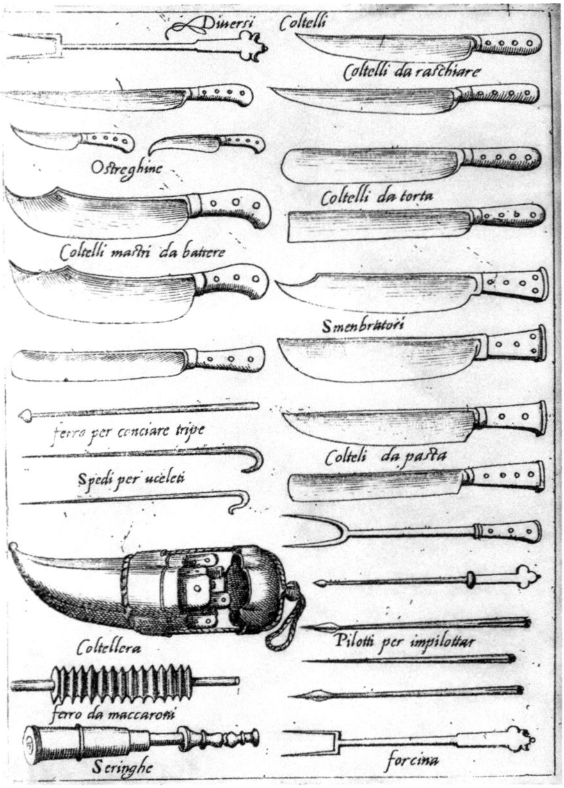

Knives of different kinds, from *Opera di M. Bartolomeo Scappi, cuoco,* Venice, Tramezzino, 1570

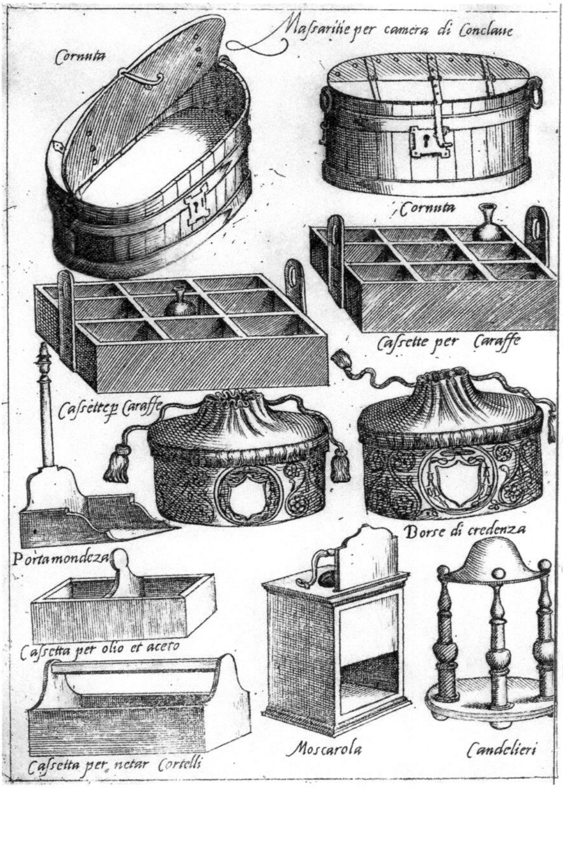

Furnishings for the conclave chamber, from *Opera di M. Bartolomeo Scappi, cuoco,* Venice, Tramezzino, 1570

Orazio Fortezza, *Plate from a set dedicated to Alvise Foscari,* c. 1560, ø 46.3 cm, London, Victoria and Albert Museum

Ceramic plate with Foscari arms, c. 1530, ø 29 cm, *Glasses and decanters with the Foscari coat of arms*

a large fork and cutting it from below with a razor-sharp knife in a series of lightning moves so the sliced meat fell neatly onto the plate below.

While this was taking place, the voices mingled in conversation, interrupted by occasional hearty laughter. A dog or two might scrabble under the table between the chair legs. The musicians played their instruments, occasionally accompanied by singers. The cupbearer continued to pour wine. Dishes of food were set on the table and the guests would help themselves.

However, these banquets were rare events. It was common for forms of lunching and dining that were not used in the city to be tried out in the country. Once again, we have to rely on the paintings by Pozzoserrato, which show how the custom of eating in the open air gradually spread, seated under pergolas that created a privileged and elegant space, set apart from the surrounding countryside. Chess or card games were then introduced to prolong the pleasure of spending time outdoors, a pastime that in the mid-sixteenth century was still waiting to be discovered.

In the late morning on 6 August 1574 a fanfare of trumpets was heard from the west of the house. An unusual crowd had gathered on the left bank of the Brenta. On the opposite bank, in front of the house, there were a handful of men commanded by the Capitano of Gambarare and an unspecified number of officials from the Venetian Signoria who were trying to stop boats filled with onlookers from mooring at the side of the canal.

The approaching procession was escorting the young Henri of Valois, King of Poland, who – having already spent two weeks in Venice – had decided to embark in full pomp on the journey that would lead him in triumph to Paris where he would be crowned King of France. Henri of Valois was the third and last son of Catherine de' Medici, and he was accompanied by some of Italy's leading princes and a retinue of four hundred.

Not many of the courtiers landed when they arrived at the house built, as Palladio says, "on the

Venetian School, *The Wedding Feast at Cana*,
16th century, Private collection

Paris Bordon, *Chess players*, 1540, Berlin, Gemäldegalerie

The title of this painting by Vittore Carpaccio might equally be "waiting", or perhaps more appropriately "boredom". That the two Venetian women shown in the painting are ladies (and not two courtesans, as was once suggested) is demonstrated by their "large pearl" necklaces.
They are clearly bored by the long hours of waiting because their husbands have chosen to go hunting ducks in the lagoon rather than remain with them.
This ironical nature of the scene suggests that the panel on which the painting has been executed might well come from the "cupboard" used in the villa to keep the husband's bows and arrows.

Vittore Carpaccio, *Two Venetian Ladies (Hunting on the Lagoon),* 1490–1495, Venice, Museo Correr and Los Angeles, Getty Museum

Portrait of Henri III de Valois, c. 1578, Private collection

Brenta". The house was simply not large enough to accommodate such a large concourse of people. However, following the same etiquette that he had used to welcome the king to his house "on the bend of the Canal" in Venice (now the seat of Venice University), Alvise Foscari (who was at the time in charge of the Republic's fortresses) stood on the banks of the Brenta to receive the young sovereign. When they approached the house, Foscari let his royal guest lead the way up one of the external staircases. Henri was, as usual, followed by some of his *mignons* from whom he refused to be separated. On reaching the portico, he turned to look out, framed by the large doorway behind him as another fanfare of trumpets was sounded. It was Elisabetta who then welcomed him into the house.

The reason for this visit by Henri de Valois was not that the king wished to stop for refreshments but rather he wished to thank Alvise for the hospitality which he and his retinue had enjoyed while they stayed in the Venetian family home, the large house that had been built by Doge Francesco Foscari.

And perhaps there was also another reason. Henri wanted to meet the architect who, two weeks earlier, had erected that large loggia at the Lido, where he had been received on the edge of the lagoon by the Venetian Signoria, and the triumphal arch through which he had stepped with some emotion to start the last stretch of his journey across St Mark's Basin to the Ducal Palace and from there, followed by dozens of gondolas, up the Grand Canal.

There is no question that the house "on the Brenta" would have been decked out for the occasion with all the most precious ornaments and furnishings that Alvise and Elisabetta possessed. However, the king cannot have stayed longer than was necessary. That evening he arrived in Padua and spent the night in the grand Palazzo dell'Arena (the Roman arena, of course), formerly owned by the Scrovegni rulers, which had recently been admirably restored (according to Francesco Sansovino) by Piero Foscari, a relative of our Alvise.

Andrea Vicentino, *The Venetian Entrance of Henri III de Valois, King of France,* 1593, Venice, Doge's Palace

Palma the Younger, *The Arrival of Henri III de Valois at Ca' Foscari,* 1593–1595, Dresden, Gemäldegalerie

The chapel and Palace of the Scrovegni (engraving from A. Buzzacarini, 1842)

Vincenzo Coronelli, "Transcription of the stone plaque above the main door to the piano nobile of Villa Foscari commemorating the arrival of Henri III", from *La Brenta, quasi borgo ecc*, Venice, 1711

For the religious services that Henri de Valois attended with particular devotion every morning to expiate the sins of the previous night, he would have made his way at dawn to the chapel right beside the palace that was already famous for Giotto's frescos, which covered the walls, and for its ceiling in lapis lazuli, a display of wealth that no other European ruler could have equalled.

To commemorate this royal visit to their *case di villa,* above the entrance door Alvise and Elisabetta would later have painted – in exquisite understatement – the scene from Ovid's myths in which Philemon and Baucis – a couple who were very much in love with one another – welcomed Jupiter, the king of the gods, to their humble abode and offered him a meal with as much zeal and care as they could in keeping with their poverty.

Battista Zelotti, *Jupiter and Mercury welcomed by Philemon and Baucis,* Villa Foscari

Endnotes

1 Likewise, there was only one outdoor location in the city that could be called "Piazza": that was the area overlooked by the Palace and the Chapel containing the remains of St Mark the Evangelist.
2 A. Palladio, *I Quattro Libri dell'Architettura,* Venice De' Franceschi, 1570, Libro Secondo, cap. II, p. 3 [**77**]. All English translations are based on Andrea Palladio, *The Four Books of Architecture,* trans. Robert Tavernor and Richard Schofield, Cambridge Mass.: The MIT Press, 2002. The bold page number in square brackets refers to the page of the English translation.
3 *Ibidem.* Palladio insists on this concept, stressing that "if they [the houses] are not suitable their chances of praise would be very slight and they would deserve the harshest criticism".
4 A. Palladio, *I Quattro Libri,* cit., Libro Secondo, cap. XIII, p. 46 [**123**].
5 Leon Battista Alberti had been much more explicit in this respect, when he wrote – in his book *On Buildings* – that "the family is made up of the husband, the wife, the children, the grandparents, and those who live with them, being at their service, and namely administrators, domestic servants, slaves. It can also be said that the guests form part of the family." L.B. Alberti, *De Re Aedificatoria,* Florence, 1452, V, cap. XVII.
6 A. Palladio, *I Quattro Libri,* cit., Libro Secondo, cap. XII, p. 47 [**122**].
7 A. Palladio, *I Quattro Libri,* cit., Libro Secondo, cap. XIV, p. 47 [**124**]. Elsewhere, I have tried to explain the reasons why there are two "beautiful and decorated" storeys in some Palladian buildings in suburban settings – such as the buildings at Piombino Dese and Montagnana", see A. Foscari, *Andrea Palladio. Unbuilt Venice,* trans. Lucinda Byatt, Baden, Lars Müller Publishers, 2010, pp. 103–108.
8 *Ibidem.*
9 A. Palladio, *I Quattro Libri,* cit., Libro Secondo, cap. III, p. 4 [**84**]; also in cap. XVII, p. 66 [**147**].
10 A. Palladio, *I Quattro Libri,* cit., Libro Secondo, cap. XIV, p. 47 [**124**].
11 A. Palladio, *I Quattro Libri,* cit., Libro Secondo, cap. III, p. 4 [**84**] and also in cap. XIV, p. 65 [**143**].
12 A. Palladio, *I Quattro Libri,* cit., Libro Secondo, cap. XIV, p. 47 [**124**].
13 Palladio enhances this concept – along with others – "in all the [his] buildings for farms" by building "a tympanum [*frontespicio*] on the front facade where the principal doors are, because tympanums accentuate the entrance of the house and contribute greatly to the grandeur and magnificence of the building [...]

furthermore, they are perfectly suited to the insignia or arms of the patrons [*edificatori*]." A. Palladio, *I Quattro Libri*, cit., Libro Secondo, Cap XVI, p. 69 [**147**].

14 A. Palladio, *I Quattro Libri*, cit., Libro Secondo, p. 50 [**128**].

15 A. Palladio, *I Quattro Libri*, cit., Libro Secondo, Cap XIV, p. 47 [**124**].

16 *Ibidem*.

17 *Ibidem*.

18 A. Palladio, *I Quattro Libri*, cit., Libro Secondo, cap. XIV, p. 52 [**130**].

19 *Ibidem*.

20 A. Palladio, *I Quattro Libri*, cit., Libro Secondo, cap. II, p. 3 [**78**].

21 A. Palladio, *I Quattro Libri*, cit., Libro Secondo, cap. II, p. 45 [**77–78**].

22 A. Palladio, *I Quattro Libri*, cit., Libro Secondo, cap. XII, p. 45 [**121**].

23 A. Palladio, *I Quattro Libri*, cit., Libro Secondo, p. 50 [**128**].

24 "I am in favour – Palladio writes – of putting the cellars, the wood stores, the pantries, the kitchens, the smaller dining rooms, the laundries, the ovens, and the other things essential for daily life in the lowest part of the building, which I put partly underground", see A. Palladio, *I Quattro Libri*, cit., Libro Secondo, cap. II, p. 3 [**78**].

25 *Ibidem*.

26 *Ibidem*.

27 A. Palladio, *I Quattro Libri*, cit., Libro Secondo, cap. XII, p. 45 [**121**].

28 A. Palladio, *I Quattro Libri*, cit., Libro Secondo, cap. II, p. 3 [**78**].

29 A study undertaken by Micaela Dal Corso on the writing – for the most part, damaged over the years – on the walls of the central room of the upper floor bears out the use of this area as a "granary". Words such as grape, potatoes, grain and "formenton" or buckwheat can be glimpsed. Further confirmation is provided by minute fragments of beans and grains in a floor cavity which was inspected during maintenance work.

30 A. Palladio, *I Quattro Libri*, cit., Libro Secondo, cap. XIV, p. 47 [**124**].

31 For a clearer understanding of this development, consider the interval that elapsed between the date of his early "case di villa" and the publication of his treatise (1570).

32 At a later phase, these windowsills were fitted with balustrades that allowed the air to ventilate the floor level. This might indicate that by the end of the eighteenth century these "rooms above" were also used as granaries.

33 On the construction of these dormers, see A. Foscari, "Il disegno della fabbrica costruita in Malcontenta che

Palladio pubblica nel suo Libro Secondo", in *Arte / Documento,* n. 26, Venice, Marcianum Press, 2010, pp. 177–183.
34 L. Dolce, *Dialogo di M. Lodovico Dolce della institution delle donne: da lui stesso in questa quarta impressione riueduto, e di piu utili cose ampliato, & con la tauola delle cose piu degne di memoria,* Venice, Gabriel Giolito de' Ferrari, p. 12.
35 A. Palladio, *I Quattro Libri,* cit., Libro Secondo, cap. II, p. 4 [**78**].
36 *Ibidem.*
37 On the "fraterna", a business partnership among brothers that was typical of many Venetian enterprises, see F. Porcellini, *Tractatus de duobus fratribus,* Venice, 1559, and G. Micalosio, *Tractatus de Fratribus,* Venice, 1736. On the "fraterna" as an institution in Venetian society, also see M. Ferro, *Dizionario del diritto comune e veneto ecc.,* Venice, 1779, pp. 276–278.
38 In the house by the Brenta built for the Foscari brothers, this arrangement was introduced following Nicolò's death. See A. Foscari, *Frescos within Palladio's Architecture. Malcontenta 1557–1575,* trans. Lucinda Byatt, Zurich, Lars Müller Publishers, 2013, pp. 114ff.
39 A. Palladio, *I Quattro Libri,* cit., Libro Secondo, cap. II, p. 4 [**78**].
40 *Ibidem.*
41 *Ibidem.*
42 *Ibidem.*
43 A. Palladio, *I Quattro Libri,* cit., Libro Secondo, cap. XII, p. 45 [**121**].
44 These details, which appear, as was mentioned, in the fresco decorations for the two rooms, lead us to suppose that in the Veneto it was not customary for other men, who might be termed bodyguards, to sleep in the owner's room – as they did in Cardinal Farnese's room in Caprarola.
45 A. Palladio, *I Quattro Libri,* cit., Libro Secondo, cap. XII, p. 45 [**121**].
46 A. Palladio, *I Quattro Libri,* cit., Libro Secondo, cap. XII, p. 47 [**124**]. This practice of inviting guests to stay overnight is also confirmed by the short description of the villa built for Marco Repeta "who gladly receives all those who come to visit him". This is a house that has often attracted the attention of scholars "the part lived in by the owner and that for the farm are on the same level" and are symmetrical in plan, while the centre of the house is empty (a solution that several scholars have attributed to a daring and precise ideological conviction). See A. Palladio, *I Quattro Libri,* cit., Libro Secondo, p. 61 [**139**].
47 A. Palladio, *I Quattro Libri,* cit., Libro Secondo, cap. XII, p. 45 [**121**].
48 *Ibidem.*
49 *Ibidem.*

50 On this subject, see: E. Narducci, *Le ambiguità della "amicizia"*, introduction to M.T. Cicero, *L'amicizia,* Classici Greci e Latini, Milan, Rizzoli, 2010, pp. 5–57, and especially pp. 8–28.

51 A. Palladio, *I Quattro Libri,* cit., Libro Secondo, cap. XII, p. 47 [**139**].

52 For example, there are no "dining-tables" in the sixteenth century. In view of the strikingly small dimensions of the "small rooms", the thought comes to mind that when he was visited by his "virtuous friends", the owner would eat at a table that was laid for him in the adjoining square room, where the friends would stay and converse.

53 On this last point, it is worth mentioning the peremptory view of an intellectual, Giovan Maria Memmo. In a treatise he wrote: "I am heartily in favour of the habit [...] of not allowing children into the father's presence until they have been well brought up and well mannered." See G.M. Memmo, *Dialogo... nel quale dopo alcune filosofiche dispute si forma un perfetto prencipe et una perfetta repubblica e parimente un senatore, un cittadino, un soldato et un mercatante,* Venice, G. Giolito de' Ferrari, 1563, p. 23.

54 A. Palladio, *I Quattro Libri,* cit., Libro Secondo, cap. II, p. 4 [**78**].

55 A certain warmth is also assured in these small rooms by the fact that the flue for the kitchen fire, located in the basement, was housed within the interior wall of this room. It is worth noting that these flues – when built inside walls of limited thickness – were very shallow (generally just 13 cm in depth) but quite wide (60–80 cm).

56 D. Romoli, *La singolare dottrina,* 1598, Venice, Tramezzino, 1598, p. 9.

57 A. Palladio, *I Quattro Libri,* cit., Libro Secondo, cap. XII, p. 45 [**121**].

58 A. Palladio, *I Quattro Libri,* cit., Libro Secondo, cap. II, p. 4 [**78**].

59 Richard Norris, Victoria and Albert Museum, drawing E 1516–1917.

60 A. Palladio, *I Quattro Libri,* cit., Libro Secondo, cap. II, p. 4 [**78**].

61 A. Palladio, *I Quattro Libri,* cit., Libro Secondo, cap. XII, p. 45 [**121**].

62 The Palladian building (*fabbrica*) stood, solemn and alone, in this setting, like a white metaphysical volume. The trees which were planted around this house from 1924 onwards – as well as indicating a different culture of the landscape – also serve to screen the view of the disorderly urbanisation that has spread around it.

63 Indeed, the many windows on the southern end of the central hall in this house are not fitted with shutters.

64 Talking about the white paintings he had produced in the autumn of 1951, Robert Rauschenberg would later say in an interview: "I always thought of the white paintings as being [...] hypersensitive. So one could look at them and see how many people were in the room by the shadows cast, or what time of day it was."
65 A. Foscari, *Frescos,* cit.
66 A. Palladio, *I Quattro Libri,* cit., Libro Secondo, cap. II, p. 3 [**77**].
67 A. Foscari, *Tumult and Order. Malcontenta 1924–1939,* trans. Lucinda Byatt, Zurich, Lars Müller Publishers, 2012, p. 139.
68 The limited size of this opening and its unique nature depend on the fact that outside the stairs leading to the portico butt against the external walls of the house, and the portico itself has a large base.
69 Cfr. A. Palladio, *I Quattro Libri,* cit., Libro Secondo, p. 50 [**128**].
70 B. Scappi, *Opera di M. Bartolomeo Scappi. Divisa in sei libri,* Venice, Tramezzino, 1570, Plate XIXa.
71 Alberti had recommended that food should not be carried (from the kitchen) to the table over too long a distance or along an awkward route, *De Re Aedificatoria,* cit.
72 A. Palladio, *I Quattro Libri,* cit., Libro Secondo, p. 4 [**79**].
73 These vents "that let out at the top of the house" rise up "from the bottom of the pit through the thickness of the walls". See *Ibidem.*
74 For example, at Villa Cornaro in Piombino Dese.
75 B. Scappi, *Opera di M. Bartolomeo Scappi,* cit., Plate XXIIIa.
76 *I Quattro libri della famiglia.* The first three books were written by L.B. Alberti in Rome between 1433 and 1434; the fourth was completed in Florence in 1440.
77 *I Quattro libri della famiglia,* Rome, 1434, Libro Terzo, http://www.vicoacitillo.it/biblio/familia.pdf, p. 158 (accessed 02/07/2019). The English translation is by Renée Neu Watkins: *Leon Battista Alberti, The Family in Renaissance Florence: I Libri della Famiglia, Book Three,* Columbia, University of South Carolina Press, 1969, p. 56.
78 A. Palladio, *I Quattro Libri,* cit., Libro Secondo, cap. II, p. 46 [**123**].
79 *Ibidem.*
80 A. Palladio, *I Quattro Libri,* cit., Libro Primo, p. 52 [**57**].
81 *Ibidem.*
82 See G. Gullino, "Foscari, Alvise," *Dizionario Biografico degli Italiani,* vol. 49 (1997).
83 Alvise Foscari was Capitano at Bergamo from 1569 to Oct. 1570; Provveditore alle Fortezze at various times (7 Oct. 1570–31 March 1571; 2 April 1573–1 March 1574; 12 May 1579–31 March 1580; 7 Oct. 1581–30 Sept. 1582; 17 May–30 Sept. 1584; 5 Oct. 1585–30 Sept. 1586; 3 April 1590–31 March 1591); then Savio alla Mercanzia (2 April

1571–31 Dec. 1572; 26 June 1597–25 June 1598); and a member of the Council of Ten and its executive Zonta (1572–1573; 1579–1580; 1583–1584). He was Podestà of Brescia from September 1575. In 1578 he was Provveditore alle Spese Superflue and Conservatore delle Leggi. For all subsequent offices, see G. Gullino, "Foscari, Alvise," cit.
84 This is how Palladio describes riding equipment and tackle: A. Palladio, *I Quattro Libri,* cit., Libro Secondo, cap. II, p. 4 [**78**].
85 A. Palladio, *I Quattro Libri,* cit., Libro Secondo, p. 3 [**78**].
86 A. Gallo, *Le vinti giornate dell'agricoltura, et de' piaceri della villa ecc.,* Venice, Borgomineri al Segno di San Giorgio, 1584.
87 See A. Foscari, "Qualche notizia intorno a Jacopo Foscari di Nicolò (1507–1543)", in G. Foscari (ed.), *Prima di Andrea Palladio. La formazione di un possedimento non molto lungi dalle Gambarare,* Venice, La Malcontenta, 2005, pp. XXV–XXXI.
88 A. Palladio, *I Quattro Libri,* cit., Libro Secondo, p. 50 [**128**].
89 A. Palladio, *I Quattro Libri,* cit., Libro Secondo, cap. I, p. 3 [**77**].
90 A. Foscari, *Tumult and Order,* cit., p. 92
91 E. Forssman, *Visible Harmony, Palladio's Villa Foscari at Malcontenta,* Stockholm, The Swedish Museum of Architecture, 1973.
92 When translating and commenting on Vitruvius' texts on music, Daniele Barbaro does not fail to note: "if I were to discuss Music, I would order it differently" ["se io havaria trattare della Musica, io la ordinerei altramente"]. D. Barbaro, *I dieci libri ecc.,* Libro V, p. 219.
93 G. Zarlino, *Istitutioni armoniche ecc.,* Venice, Francesco de' Franceschi, 1558, facs. N.J. Gregg Press, 1966, II, 9, p. 75.
94 *Ibidem.*
95 Above the other two doors – the ones leading into the large rooms – we find Bellona, the art of war, and Poetry, indicating the apartments of Nicolò and Alvise respectively. The figure of Poetry was chosen for the apartment used by Alvise because at the time when the paintings were commissioned he was Conservatore of the Accademia degli Uniti. For more on this subject, see A. Foscari, *Frescos,* cit., p. 46.
96 B. Castiglione, *Il libro del Cortigiano,* Venice, 1528 (edition published in Milan, E. Sonzogno, 1947), p. 25. The English translation of this passage from Book I, chapter 46, is taken from *The Book of the Courtier,* edited by Daniel Javitch, New York, W.W. Norton, 2002, p. 55.
97 *Ibidem.*
98 D. Barbaro, *I dieci libri ecc.,* Cap V, p. 227. The English translation of this passage is taken from Kim

Williams (ed.), *Daniele Barbaro's Vitruvius of 1567,* Cham, Birkhäuser, 2019, pp. 369–70.
99 A. Palladio, *I Quattro Libri,* cit., Libro Primo, p. 45 [**121**].
100 A. Palladio, *I Quattro Libri,* cit., Libro Secondo, p. 72 [**150**].
101 B. Castiglione, *Il libro del Cortigiano,* cit., p. 25 [**55**] More generally on this topic see S. Lorenzetti, *Musica e identità nobiliare nell'Italia del Rinascimento: educazione, mentalità, immaginario,* Florence, L.S. Olschki, 2003, especially Chapter 3.
102 G. Zarlino, *Istitutioni armoniche ecc.,* cit., p. 75.
103 *Ibidem.*
104 I am particularly grateful to Professor Francesco Rossi of Università Ca' Foscari Venice for having kindly identified these instruments.
105 S. Zuccolo, *La Pazzia del Ballo,* Padua, Jacopo Fabriano, 1549.
106 R. Corso, *Dialogo del Ballo di m. Rinaldo Corso,* Venice, Sigismondo Bordogna, 1555.
107 See A. Pontremoli and P. Rocca, *La danza a Venezia nel Rinascimento,* Vicenza, Neri Pozza Editore, 1993, Chapter "La danza nel Rinascimento", especially pp. 88ff.
108 *Ibidem.*
109 F. Sansovino, *Venetia, citta nobilissima et singolare,* Venice, Iacomo Sansovino, 1581, Libro X, p. 401.
110 Written between 1496 and 1533.
111 See A. Foscari, "Festeggiamenti in Ca' Foscari per le nozze di Ferigo il giorno 2 maggio 1513", in *Ludica, annali di storia e civiltà del gioco,* n. 13–14, Rome, Viella, 2007–2008 (2011), pp. 38–49.
112 See A. Foscari, "Sulla riva del Canal Grande, a San Simeon Piccolo. La 'struttura teatrale' in cui ha debuttato a Venezia il Ruzzante", in M.A. Chiari Moretto Wiel and A. Gentili (eds), *L'attenzione e la critica. Scritti di storia dell'arte in memoria di Terisio Pignatti,* Padua, Il Poligrafo, 2008, pp. 101–113.
113 D. Romoli, *La singolare dottrina,* cit.
114 B. Scappi, *Opera di M. Bartolomeo Scappi,* cit.
115 See note 101.
116 G. della Casa, *Trattato di messer Giovanni della Casa... cognominato Galatheo overo de costumi ecc.,* Venice, Nicolò Bevilacqua, 1558.

Image Credits

Cover image, p. 5 © 2010 Christie's Images Limited
pp. 8–9 Pinacoteca del Castello Sforzesco, Milano, © Comune di Milano tutti i diritti riservati
p. 10 © 2019, Archivio Fotografico, Fondazione Musei Civici di Venezia
pp. 18–19 Photo: Marie-Pierre Morel
p. 21 Photo: Matthias Schaller
pp. 22–23 © 2019, Museo National Thyssen-Bornemisza/Scala, Firenze
pp. 26–27 © Antonio Foscari
p. 28 Photo: Marie-Pierre Morel
p. 31 © 2019, Archivio Fotografico, Fondazione Musei Civici di Venezia
pp. 32–33 Photo: Matthias Schaller
pp. 34–35 Photo: Matthias Schaller
pp. 40–41 [Public domain], via Wikimedia Commons
p. 42 © 2019, Musei Civici di Treviso
p. 44 © 2019, Photo Scala, Florence
p. 47 [Public domain], via Wikimedia Commons
p. 48 [Public domain], via Wikimedia Commons
p. 49 Stiftung Preußische Schlösser und Gärten Berlin-Brandenburg/Photographer: Gerhard Murza
pp. 50–51 Photo: Matthias Schaller
p. 52–53 Photo: Matthias Schaller
p. 54 Photo: Marie-Pierre Morel
p. 56–57 © 2019, Bottega delle Arti, Padova
p. 60 Photo: Lord Snowdon
p. 62–63 Photo: François Halard
p. 64 © 2019, Foto Scala, Florence
pp. 66–67 [Public domain], via Wikimedia Commons
p. 69 Photo: Osvaldo Boehm
p. 70 Photo: Antonio Foscari
p. 73 Photo: Mauro Galligani
pp. 76–77 Photo: François Halard
p. 79 Photo: Antonio Foscari
p. 83 Photo: Matthias Schaller
pp. 84–85 [Public domain], via Wikimedia Commons
pp. 94–95 [Public domain], via Wikimedia Commons
p. 98 © Victoria and Albert Museum, London
pp. 102–103 © 2019, Photo Scala, Florence/bpk, Bildagentur für Kunst, Kultur und Geschichte, Berlin
p. 105 [Public domain], via Wikimedia Commons
pp. 108–109 © 2019, Archivio Fotografico, Fondazione Musei Civici di Venezia
© 2019, Photo Scala, Florence/bpk, Bildagentur für Kunst, Kultur und Geschichte, Berlin
pp. 112–113 Photo: Matthias Schaller
pp. 126–127 Photo: Ferigo Foscari

Antonio Foscari, architect, has been professor of architectural history at the IUAV University of Venice for many years. He has focused his research on the history of Italian Renaissance architecture.

Foscari is Vice President of the Andrea Palladio International Centre for Architectural Studies. From 2005 to 2011 he was a member of the board of the Louvre. He has been awarded the titles of Chevalier des Arts et des Lettres and Légion d'Honneur by the French Republic.

Foscari has published extensively on Italian Renaissance Architecture. In 1983 he published *Armonia e Conflitti. La chiesa di San Francesco della Vigna nella Venezia del '500* (Einaudi) with Manfredo Tafuri. On Palladio, he has authored the following monographs: *Andrea Palladio Unbuilt Venice* (2010); *Tumult and Order. Malcontenta 1924–1939* (2012); and *Frescos within Palladio's Architecture. Malcontenta 1557–1575* (2013), all published by Lars Müller Publishers. At present Antonio Foscari is working on a publication on *Andrea Palladio and Palazzo Ducale in Venezia.*

Evening shot of the northern facade of Villa Foscari.
The exterior and interior are lit by candles. (25 May 2019)

Living with Palladio
in the Sixteenth Century

Author: Antonio Foscari
Translations: Lucinda Byatt
Proofreading: Ian McDonald
Design: Lars Müller Publishers/Lars Müller and
Audrey Solomon
Production: Esther Butterworth
Lithography: prints professional, Berlin, Germany
Printing and binding: Graspo, Zlín, Czech Republic
Paper: Munken Polar, 130 gsm

Lars Müller Publishers is supported by the Swiss Federal Office of Culture with a structural contribution for the years 2021–2025.

Lars Müller Publishers
Pfingstweidstrasse 6
8005 Zurich
Switzerland
www.lars-mueller-publishers.com
+41 44 274 37 40

Product safety
Producer: Lars Müller Publishers GmbH
Responsible person in accordance with EU Regulation 2023/988 (GPSR): Michael Klein, sales representative,
Hub 1, DE-84149 Velden
+49 8742 964 552 2, gpsr@lars-mueller-publishers.com

ISBN 978-3-03778-638-3

Distributed in North America by ARTBOOK | D.A.P.
www.artbook.com

Printed in the Czech Republic